MW00574832

Your

TAROT
COURT

ABOUT THE AUTHOR

Ethony is a tarot reader and author who loves to create more than sleep. She is the creator of the Bad Bitches Tarot, the Awakened Soul Oracle, the Prince Lenormand Oracle, and the Money Magic Manifestation Cards. She is the Headmistress at www.TarotReadersAcademy.com where she teaches and mentors tarot professionals and students through the courses available there. Ethony is a very proud mother to a wonderful son and has the best family and friends any person could ask for.

ETHONY DAWN

Your
TAROT
COURT
{READ ANY DECK WITH CONFIDENCE}

Llewellyn Publications
Woodbury, Minnesota

FIRST EDITION
First Printing, 2019

Cover design by Kevin R. Brown
Cover tarot card art is from Llewellyn's Classic Tarot by Eugene Smith
Editing by Brian R. Erdrich
Illustrations from The Bad Bitches Tarot © 2015 by Ethony Dawn are used with permission, no further reproduction allowed.
Illustrations from The Steampunk Tarot by Aly Fell and Barbara Moore © 2012 used with permission, no further reproduction allowed.
Illustrations from Everyday Witch Tarot by Deborah Blake and Elisabeth Alba © 2012, reproduced with permission from Llewellyn Publications, no further reproduction allowed.
Illustrations from Tarot Mucha © 2015 by Giulia Massaglia, Barbara Nosenzo, Lunaea Weatherstone, and Massimiliano Filador are used with permission from LoScarabeo, Torino Italy, no further reproduction allowed.
Illustrations from The Triple Goddess Tarot by Jaymi Elford and Franco Rivolli © 2017 are used with permission from LoScarabeo, Torino Italy, no further reproduction allowed.

Llewellyn Publications is a registered trademark of Llewellyn Worldwide Ltd.

Library of Congress Cataloging-in-Publication Data (Pending)
ISBN: 987-0-7387-5865-7

Llewellyn Worldwide Ltd. does not participate in, endorse, or have any authority or responsibility concerning private business transactions between our authors and the public.
All mail addressed to the author is forwarded but the publisher cannot, unless specifically instructed by the author, give out an address or phone number.
Any internet references contained in this work are current at publication time, but the publisher cannot guarantee that a specific location will continue to be maintained. Please refer to the publisher's website for links to authors' websites and other sources.

Llewellyn Publications
A Division of Llewellyn Worldwide Ltd.
2143 Wooddale Drive
Woodbury, MN 55125-2989
www.llewellyn.com

Printed in the United States of America

Dedicated to my son, my ray of sunshine, Dominic.
Thank you for letting me see the world through your eyes.

CONTENTS

LIST OF PRACTICUMS AND TAROT EXERCISES

INTRODUCTION

You have entered the world of intrigue, power, strong wills, and changing faces. History has shown that the royal court can be a dangerous place where people hold their cards close to their chest (no pun intended) and missteps can lead to grave misfortune at the hand of powerful players. That may be a clue as to why the court cards are so hard to understand when they appear in a tarot reading. People are always changing and wear many masks.

When I first started to study the tarot seriously, I would have readings where the court cards came up all of the time. It was incredibly frustrating, but it did force me to learn how to connect and communicate with these important cards in the tarot.

The court cards can be some of the hardest to understand in the deck. I decided to write this book and these exercises to provide you with a further understanding of the cards so that you won't remove them from your decks (yeah I know you are out there) and the colour will not drain from your face when you flip over a court card. Fear not, the court cards are there to help you better understand yourself and the people around you. They can do this by identifying limiting patterns in your personal and professional lives and allowing you to lean into your strengths. Even after working through this book, the tarot court may still confuse you from time to time, but a little mystery is a good thing.

One of the amazing things about the tarot is that you never stop learning, because there are so many layers to the cards. The meaning and experience of the cards can change depending on the question you ask, the position the card is in, and what cards are next to each other. We all bring our own history and set of experiences to the table as well, which is another layer added to a tarot reading. This is why it can take years to become a proficient tarot reader and a certain knack for being a good tarot reader.

This book will help you explore the court cards in more than one way. This really is a "getting to know your court" book. So the fact that there is more than one definition given or question posed is purposefully done.

The more you work with the tarot, the more you will learn and become comfortable, recognising when each card means a certain thing.

There are a number of exercises in this book and I highly recommend that you use a notebook or blank journal to record your journey. I have a number of notebooks that I use for the tarot and I always date the entries so that I can look back and reflect. Being a visual learner, I really enjoy a brightly coloured journal and have decoupaged my own many times for my notes. Use whatever medium works best for you.

When it comes to selecting a tarot deck to work with try to find a deck with beautiful, detailed, engaging court cards, make sure that the images resonate with you. The more you like the look of the cards or the more they speak to you, the better your experience will be. Don't be worried if you have a less than positive reaction to some of the cards. That is normal. For example, I find that sometimes the ugliest card of the court is the Queen of Swords, and she is my significator card! I still love her stern face anyway.

> **Tarot Jargon**—*significator*—This is a card that signifies the person the reading is about. This can be yourself, your client or a third party. It can help anchor the reading so that the outcome is clearer and specifically about that person. For readings where you use a significator, you do not need to interpret the significator cards; they are there to anchor a reading and hold a representational energy.

The most common feedback I have had over the years from students and fellow tarot readers is that when a court card appears in a reading, it is hard to ascertain whether it represents a person in the querent's life or an aspect of the querent themselves. Or to be really tricky, both. They can be complicated because people are complicated.

> **Tarot Jargon**—*querent*—The querent is the person the tarot reading is for, the person asking the questions of the cards. It can be yourself if you are reading for personal development and knowledge.

My way of seeing the tarot court is that they are a representation of the archetypes in our lives and the way we interact with the people in our lives. You will know who they are when they arrive in a tarot reading **through the behaviours and interactions the querent is experiencing in their situation.** This statement is bolded for your benefit as this is important information to remember throughout the rest of the book. If there is just one thing that you take from this whole book when you are looking at identifying the tarot court in your tarot reading, it is paying attention to the behaviours and interactions at play.

Asking what behaviours and interactions you are experiencing and/or seeing in your life will allow you to get to the heart of the tarot court cards at play, and you will know through these if they are the people around you or if they are aspects of yourself. When you are reading the tarot for another person, you can describe the tarot court cards that are in the reading and ask them if any of the behaviours and interactions ring true to their situation or if it is how they are acting and reacting.

Even if every sixth sense you have is telling you that your querent is one of the court cards, remember not everyone is ready or willing to see themselves in a mirror, which is essentially what the tarot is; a spiritual, archetypal, symbolic mirror. When a court card arrives in a reading and it is a positive, vibrant addition, then people are more likely to want to associate themselves with the card. It can be harder to navigate the people and personalities of the tarot when they are reflecting unattractive and difficult behaviours.

Fear not if you are a tarot reader who is just beginning your journey with the tarot and the tarot court by extension. You will cultivate your skills over time and with practice. Every tarot reader, student, professional, and adept has been told they are wrong or at least not 100 percent correct at some point in their journey. If they deny this, they are full of shit. So the tarot court cards are a little elusive, but don't let that scare you off. They also hold so much knowledge and opportunity to understand ourselves and the people in our lives.

Your Tarot Court is a book that will help you peel back the layers of the tarot court cards and get to know them all deeply and personally. Each chapter presents you with information you can use as beautiful building blocks that will round out your knowledge of these elusive characters and ensure that these tricky bastards don't trip up your readings ever again.

This book has been written so that the information presented in each chapter is a building block. These are meant to be used together. Each time you learn something new about a tarot court card member, you are adding another layer to your building knowledge. The book is designed to be read in order and the exercises in the book are placed to help you put the information in the relating chapters into use.

There is a section at the back where you are given quick glance cheat sheets on each of the tarot court members, which can be used to refresh your memory if you need to confirm key information or themes—or if you just like to read your books backward. The information presented in those cheat sheets will make a lot more sense if the book has been read in order, but it is also comprehensible enough if you have a good working foundation of the tarot already. So basically, read the pretty words I wrote for you.

~ One ~
THE STRUCTURE OF THE TAROT

I believe that the way we experience and view the tarot is personal and evolving. There are many different ways to see the structure of the tarot. I want to share with you how I work with the tarot's structure to give some foundation for the rest of the book. This structure holds that the tarot has three parts: the major arcana, the minor arcana, and the tarot court.

THE MAJOR ARCANA

The major arcana consists of twenty-two named cards in the tarot. I view the major arcana as representing the archetypes of the divine. These are the BIG lessons that we may never fully understand. They have massive amounts of collective consciousness attached to them as spiritual beings and are cross-cultural in energy, if not by name. They are archetypal representations of our collective consciousness. Those consistent, directing patterns of influence are an inherent part of human nature and experience. Each major arcana card is given a number, a place in a specific well-thought-out order, and a title that links the card to its meaning and deeper lesson.

THE MINOR ARCANA

The minor arcana is divided into four elemental and symbolic suits. Each suit starts with the ace and the completion of the suit is at the ten. I view the minor arcana as the way we live and experience the major arcana in our everyday lives. Through the images and meanings of the minor arcana, we are bringing the divine, the big picture, down to our daily life. They are a reminder that everything is sacred. There are lessons we can learn in everything. It is all a reflection of the universe experiencing itself. The minor arcana show us real-world reactions, cause and effect, and situations we are likely to experience in life, love, career, and spirituality.

THE TAROT COURT

The tarot court consists of the people and personalities of the tarot and in our lives. They are also our own personal archetypes and the different roles and behaviours we display and take on in various relationships in our lives. This is where we see the tarot cards and themes interact with each other in a personal way.

The tarot court is a reflection of cultural and collective themes and parts that we consciously and subconsciously choose to play. In these cards we are able to explore the different aspects of who we are and why we may act and react a certain way. The tarot court can also teach us about the people in our lives and help us heal relationships and make the most out of the interpersonal connections we make.

EXERCISE: GETTING TO KNOW YOU

For this exercise you will need a deck of tarot cards, a notebook, and pen.

Forget what you know about the court cards (if anything) or at least come to this exercise with as much of a blank slate as you can. This exercise allows you to see the tarot court cards in a different light. If you have a new tarot deck that you have yet to work with, this is a perfect way to connect to that deck's court cards.

Select the deck that you would like to work with for this exercise and take out all of the court cards. Once that has been done, place the rest of the tarot deck aside as you will not require it for this exercise.

You can choose to shuffle the court cards, but I suggest to make it easier for you to reference your notes later by completing this exercise in order of suit (all of the cups together or all of the pages together etc.).

Now pick the first tarot court card from your pile. Write down the title of the card in your notebook and spend some time really looking at the card. Take everything in: the colours presented, the landscape of the card, facial expressions of the member of the court card, any animals or symbols present, the overall feel of the card, etc. From the list of suggested questions below, ask a couple of these of the card you've chosen. Record your answers in your tarot journal.

SUGGESTED QUESTIONS

The Pages

- What is your favourite game to play?
- What do you want to be when you grow up?
- What pet do you have?

The Knights

- Where are you going?
- What is your quest in life?
- What is your favourite travel destination?

The Queens

- What do you love?
- How do you value power?
- What is your favourite possession?

The Kings

- What do you do in your downtime?
- How do people prove their worth to you?
- What is your favourite book?

Being familiar with the actions, motivations, and ideals of the royal court can help you identify people in your tarot readings with more ease.

~ Two ~
IS THE TAROT
COURT DATED?

Tarot is pretty old, evolving from a card game in the fourteenth century in Europe to a modern tool that is used for psychic readings, counselling, divination, writing, and healing. The titles of the tarot court were plucked from history and have stood the test of time. While the tarot and society has changed key themes, the desires of people that make up our societies have largely remained the same. We all need shelter, food, love, amongst other things; we all have interpersonal relationships and are born into various institutions. I view the tarot as one of the representations of the book of life. The tarot shows many of the archetypes, situations, and lessons we are likely to experience while we are here understanding the human condition. The tarot court is part of that book of life.

The tarot court are all stations of royalty, and in modern times, royalty is rare. Talk of kings and queens is mostly reserved for our favourite television shows, movies, and books. Modern living royal families, while still very much in the public eye, are also part of a hierarchical system that most of us aren't. This system often has its own set of rules and regulations that members are expected to uphold. They are not your average everyday people.

The reverence that went along with royalty is now extended to actors, sports stars, and social media magnates.

With titles that can seem unrelatable, there is a good argument to be made that the tarot court is redundant. What would these stuffy, out of touch people have to teach us about life anyway, right? However, I see this view as valid only if we are looking at the title and the very surface of the tarot court. Societies and cultures change with the times, and the tarot is catching up with some incredible modern interpretations and offerings, with how many of us see our daily lives with inclusive representations offered.

Another thing that these high-class titles can afford in the way of modern relevance is how they use power, as these are some powerful beings and there is nothing more alluring, sexy, and even romanticized than power. Humans are attracted to powerful people, and the tarot court can show us how we use and sometimes abuse our own power. Social manipulation, cliques, alliances, deals, and hidden motivations are all relevant today from high school to the boardroom. By embracing the tarot court and their power, we are often better at playing out our own versions of *Game of Thrones* with less horrific dispatching of key players, one would hope.

I believe we can still honour the tradition of the tarot court, while integrating new levels of knowledge and awareness of our role and place in society. There is wisdom in the tradition of the tarot court that we can include as part of our modern spirituality and lives. That is one of the wonderful things about a living spiritual tool—it can move with the times and be ageless at the same time.

~ Three ~
TITLES, GENDER
& PHYSICAL IDENTIFIERS

It is the belief of many sociologists that gender is a social construct. As members of modern society, we are assigned a gender at birth. This is something that is done to us. We do not have any say in this assignment, and from that point on, it subconsciously shapes how we are addressed and goes along with a ton of expectations about how we behave, dress, and even what we can and cannot do with our lives. Many of these circumstances are subconscious and solidly in place before we are even born. Gender assignment does not mean that it is the gender that we identify with. This is one of the reasons that the tarot court is problematic for modern tarot readers.

If we are looking at gender within traditional tarot, you will see that the tarot court was predominantly male. As a matter of fact, the entire deck historically was predominantly male. In the tarot court, the only presence of females were the queens. Queens historically were often married into their court and not, in many societies, allowed their own reign. There has been a progressive change in the tarot world where a break from tradition has allowed for a more inclusive court. One of the factors in this assignment is that the tarot evolved from a playing card game and that structure was adopted from the Tarocchi cards. The male-majority court stuck even as the tarot evolved.

Along with the titles of the tarot court, we see cultural importance given to stations of power that are held predominantly by men. While we are going to be exploring each of the archetypes of the tarot court through a lens that has no gender assignment, there are elements of gender identification that creep in through society and what is accepted and given as power. This can also limit readers who identify as male when a queen comes up in their readings. There is much that can be gained from the wisdom of those cards, but a querent may automatically disregard the card as an aspect of themselves because the image is showing someone with assumedly different body parts from them.

Some tarot decks, such as the Thoth Tarot by Aleister Crowley, have changed the titles of the tarot court, replacing the pages for princesses. Others have their own unique court systems, like the Daughters of the Moon Tarot by Ffiona Morgan that only has the Maiden, Mother, and Crone. Still other tarot decks have depicted their tarot court as more androgynous or abstract figures, allowing the tarot reader to be less bound by traditional roles and features. Examples of these are the Wild Unknown Tarot by Kim Krans and the Tarot of the Silicon Dawn by Egypt Urnash.

Representations of people of colour (most tarot decks show the tarot court as white individuals), LGBTIQ, and people with disabilities have been rare in mainstream commercial tarot, but are slowly becoming more widely available thanks to some incredible independent creators.

The tarot court cards do not have to carry out the reproductive assumptions of their title or represented age. A queen does not have to be a mother. A king does not have to be a father. A knight can be single or married with or without children. Believe it or not, freeing the tarot court of these stigmas and assignments allows us to really harness each card's true power without getting caught up with outdated models of gender and having to cross off some gender role checklist. We have long moved past the idea that you can't be a queen unless you are a mother.

The titles used in this book are the titles associated with the court cards themselves, and their accompanying pronoun may be used when discussing a specific court card. This is so that the information can be related back to the tarot card, and to give a deeper connection and understanding of the card. It is also done to avoid confusion when you are referencing outside information on the tarot court.

We can be any of the court cards in life. In fact, we are all or many of the sixteen tarot court cards in some area of our lives or at some point. It is more about how we communicate, relate, feel, and experience certain things than being born into a role within a family or assigned with a specific gender. This will be explored in greater detail in a later chapters.

It is my philosophy that the progression of the tarot court, from the page to the king, is reflective of initiations, maturing, and coming into one's power, regardless of gender, religion, background, or age. The placement of a tarot court card in the structure of the tarot does not equate a person's gender or power when you are working with the archetypes in this book. It also does not equate your querent's and/or your own gender or power when looking at the tarot court in a reading.

PHYSICAL IDENTIFIERS

Using physical identifiers when it comes to pinning the tarot court cards down is one way you can relate and read the cards. It can be problematic. Many tarot readers would have come across a chart that looks something like this:

The Wands—A red headed person

The Cups—A blonde haired person with green or blue eyes

The Pentacles—Dark featured person with dark hair colours

The Swords—Pale skin and dark hair

Identifying people through the tarot court in relation to popular documented associations is not something that is reliable in the modern day. This in no way diminishes the use of formulas that are published and well-known. If it works for you, then carry on doing it. Due to its simplistic take on personal exteriors and lack of diverse associations such as cosmetic alterations, fake tanning, hair colouring, and contact lenses it can make it difficult to pinpoint if it is a person based solely on their physical features. It is one way in which you can help make a connection to the people in your querent's life; however, I recommend not using it as the only way you do so. You may be even more successful if you use this information as a jumping-off point along with a deeper understanding of the court through this book, for example, or you could add more associations to make them well-rounded and make sense for you.

For my own personal tarot practice, I may get a flash of what the person looks like for a client. I also look deeper at the court cards based on my client's personality and how it connects with their reading or how they interact with the world and others.

Age and the Tarot Court

Age is one way in which we can define the court. It can help you identify who the tarot court cards are in a reading. This is something that has been well discussed and explored within the tarot community. My offering to you for what age groups each of the tarot court represent is:

- *Pages*—Children—up through the age of 11
- *Knights*—Adolescents—ages 12 through 21
- *Kings and Queens*—22+, depending on how the individual identifies themselves

Beyond identifying people in the tarot court through their age alone, I invite you to view the titles in a way that reflects how we interact with our situations and the people in them. If we look at age as the only means of connecting the tarot court to the people in our lives, we are limiting their potential. Are children less valuable or less wise than adults? Do kings and queens have their lives more ordered or have a deeper understanding of life than a teenager? Rather than looking at age as the only way to know who is who in the tarot court, I view it as one of the identifiers.

~ Four ~
TAROT ELEMENTAL
ASSOCIATIONS

One of the layers of the tarot is the connection to the four directional elements. For the purposes of this book, the suits are designated using the following elements.

The Cups—Water

The Swords—Air

The Wands—Fire

The Pentacles—Earth

The strengths and weaknesses of the elements come into play with the tarot court as well as elemental chemistry. This interaction is how the elements relate to the other personalities of the cards.

Tarot readings with a high representation of any element can give you an indication of the landscape of the querent's situation. It is also important to note what elements are completely missing, as this will also give you a lot of information on how the querent can tackle the situation.

Here is a simple sample reading with a dominant element in play and how you can incorporate your understanding of the elements to help your querent while adding depth to your readings.

This three card spread is:

1. Past

2. Present

3. Future

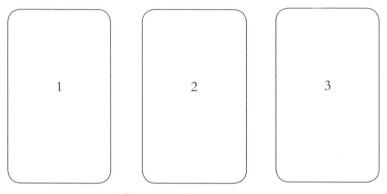

Three Card Tarot Spread

For this reading, our querent is going to be called Suzie. Suzie has come for a reading about her relationship. She is not sure why she keeps attracting the wrong person into her life. The cards that have come up for Suzie in her reading are:

1. The Page of Cups

2. The Seven of Cups

3. The Eight of Cups

The Page of Cups tells us that in the past Suzie has come to love with a lot of wide-eyed optimism and has been really focused on her relationships. With this being her sole focus, which is also supported by the other two cards being cups/emotions cards, she has created a situation where it is the end of her world when things don't turn out how she expected or wanted. The

Page of Cups can also represent someone who can be rather clingy emotion-ally and can find it hard to process and communicate their emotional needs. In other words, they throw tantrums. These are some of the factors from the past that are coming into play in the present.

The Seven of Cups in the present lets us know that she is now faced with a choice, a lot of choices, in fact. She has to decide if she is ready and willing to make a change in how she is approaching her love life and also find some ways to enrich her life outside of her relationships.

The Eight of Cups is super positive in her reading for the future. It shows that she is ready to go it alone for a while and explore who she really is. She is walking away from some prospects (represented by the cups in the tarot card), but she does so with confidence.

Suzie's elemental reading is all about her emotions, which tells us that without the other elements present, her focus on love is actually a hindrance for her finding a relationship that is healthy and sustainable. If she can bring in some earth for grounding, self-care, and practicality; fire for creativity, inner knowledge, and ability to transform; and air for logic, inspiration, and emotional intelligence, she will be well and truly beginning to round-out her amazing capacity to love. All water all the time makes for a weeping mess when things get hard.

Apply this to the tarot court and you will also see how the querent is ex-periencing and dealing with their situation and how the people in their lives are interacting with them and what is happening. This is true for both the tarot court's position—if there are a lot of queens in a reading and also their suit or if there are a lot of wands in a reading. So there can be a court station dominance as well as an elemental one represented in a reading.

The Knight of Cups is going to tackle a problem differently than the Knight of Wands. The cards hold the same position in the court hierarchy but their behaviours, reactions, actions, strengths, and weaknesses will be more aligned with their suit element. The Knight of Wands will easily take charge and will instinctively act in a situation, whereas the Knight of Cups may pause to see how they feel and what the emotional ramifications of a choice may be first.

Any court card that is a member of the wands suit will increase the energy and intensity of any of the tarot court cards of the swords suit. Fire cannot live without air—it needs it as fuel. Without air, fire will diminish. If you have a tarot reading where there are a lot of these two elements, things are very active, moving, and intense.

Pentacles and cups react with each other and increase their energy. The two heavier elements that will always look for the lowest place to settle, they support each other. If you have a tarot reading where there are a lot of these two elements, healing, and growth are themes and things may be moving a little slower.

Wands and pentacles oppose each other. Earth will put our fire. Fire cannot burn stones or soil. It is too dense. Cups and swords oppose each other. Both of these elements need a container and cannot support each other. Cups and wands also oppose each other's energy as water is a natural extinguisher to fire.

Swords and pentacles dilute each other's energy; they actually can't affect each other. There is always a little air in the soil, so they can join together, but they are also very opposite feeling, air being light and quick, and earth being slow-moving and dense.

When you have laid out all of your cards, even if you conduct a tarot reading and turn over one card at a time, take a look to see what elements are at play in the reading and where their positions are. Do the cards oppose or support each other?

When the court cards are included in the reading, contemplate how their elemental association interacts with the reading, situation, outcome, and challenges. In fact, look at all of the positions in your reading. How would they deal with their situation? What are their elemental strengths and weaknesses?

This brings us to elemental actions, something else that can be brought into consideration when looking at tarot elements, which are the combination of natural state and tarot court card power, how those elements naturally are in their environment, and the reaction of the court card.

Air—Breeze, gust, tornado, flow, and pressure

Earth—Mountains, rocks, slow, and steady

Water—Moves in a cycle, always going back to the source, permeates all things

Fire—Wild, sudden, transforming, and changing everything it touches

~ Five ~
ASTROLOGY, THE ZODIAC, AND THE COURT CARDS

Astrology is a deep, magical, and complex area of study, and in the tarot landscape today, there is a significant connection between the tarot and astrology. This was not always the case, but the game changed when famous occultist Eliphas Levi connected the tarot with astrology, the Kabbalah, and the occult in the 1800's. Metaphysical inclusions in the tarot have resonated deeply with many tarot readers and creators, and now the two are rarely separate when it comes to peoples' understanding and depictions of the cards.

It is common in this new age–inspired society to ask about a person's star sign, especially when you meet someone new and want to get the low-down on your cosmic compatibility, and most people will at least know what their sun signs are. The sun, like all of our solar system's heavenly bodies (moon, sun, and planets), move through the cycle of our twelve signs of the zodiac. A person's sun sign is what sign the sun was stationed in at the time and geographical location of their birth.

Why are sun signs so often spoken about and popular? It is because our sun sign is often the part of ourselves that we show to the outside world. Our sun signs are the conscious part of our being, the aspects of what makes us us, the parts that we are aware of consciously. It is the foundation of our complex personalities. We embody our sun sign when we meet other people for the first time and when we are at work. Our sun signs offer up some of the most dominant characteristics we have. It is often the illusion or parts of ourselves that we want people to see.

As the tarot court consists of the people and the personalities of the tarot, and therefore our lives, it is a great way to connect the reading to the people that are playing a part in our situations, lives, and often times, drama.

Your complete astrological chart will undoubtedly give you a more complete picture of the different aspects of your personality and preferences, but for the tarot court, we are going to focus on the sun sign so that you can use the information to decipher who they may be when they show up in a tarot reading, if the court card in question is someone impacting the reading or if the court card is reflecting an aspect of yourself or your querent.

The zodiac star sign is also an easy way to determine a person's significator card in the court. You can use a significator card to help zone in on your querent when conducting a reading, or just for yourself during self-reflection. If you want to use significators in a reading for another person, allow the querent to decide which court card they want to use. You can inform your querent what sign each of them are to help their choice. It is the best way to avoid assumption and embarrassment.

The astrological characteristics, keywords tied to the zodiac, correspondences and sun sign personality traits offered to you for each court card are broad so they are unlikely to tell you everything you want or need to know about a person, but it does help you narrow things down, and it is a layer of information you can gather about a person. It is another layer of identification for aiding your readings.

The pages in the tarot court do not have a fixed astrological assignment and therefore can be any of the zodiac signs in their elemental family.

THE FIRE SIGN FAMILY

The Page of Wands

Can be linked to any of the three fire astrological signs: Aries, Leo, Sagittarius. Use the lists of sun sign behaviours and keywords to help you identify which one your page may be.

The Knight of Wands

Sun Sign—Sagittarius
Born Between—23 November and 21 December
Sun Sign Keywords—Progressive, unconventional, resourceful, hot headed
Sun Sign Personality Traits

- A versatile person who can solve almost any problem in a lateral way
- A restless spirit who is always chasing something or someone out of their reach

The Queen of Wands

Sun Sign—Aries
Born Between—21 March and 20 April
Sun Sign Keywords—Impulsive, confident, rash, courageous
Sun Sign Personality Traits

- A person who likes to be in control
- Someone who owns their strong and vibrant personality

The King of Wands

Sun Sign—Leo
Born Between—23 July and 22 August
Sun Sign Keywords—Creative, commanding, generous, dramatic
Sun Sign Personality Traits

- A fun person that people are drawn to, the life of the party
- Someone who likes to keep up appearances

THE EARTH SIGN FAMILY

The Page of Pentacles

Can be linked to any of the three earth astrological signs: Taurus, Virgo, Capricorn. Use the lists of sun sign behaviours and keywords to help you identify which one your page may be.

The Knight of Pentacles

Sun Sign—Virgo
Born Between—23 August and 23 September

Sun Sign Keywords—Analytical, rational, restless, purposeful
Sun Sign Personality Traits

- Easily sets and attains goals in their career and personal lives

- A self-critical person who may be also outwardly judgemental of others

The Queen of Pentacles

Sun Sign—Capricorn
Born Between—22 December and 20 January
Sun Sun Keywords—Disciplined, organised, independent, loyal
Sun Sign Personality Traits

- A person who is more than happy to play the long game

- Will plan every minute of their vacations and has endless checklists

The King of Pentacles

Sun Sign—Taurus
Born Between—21 April and 21 May
Sun Sign Keywords—Practical, resilient, stubborn, patient
Sun Sign Personality Traits

- Resists change and often moves through times of change belligerently

- A person of few words but a lot of actions

THE WATER SIGN FAMILY

The Page of Cups

Can be linked to any of the three water astrological signs: Pisces, Cancer, Scorpio. Use the lists of sun sign behaviours and keywords to help you identify which one your page may be.

The Knight of Cups

Sun Sign—Pisces
Born Between—20 February and 20 March
Sun Sign Keywords—Spiritual, imaginative, sensitive, ever changing
Sun Sign Personality Traits

- Someone whose emotions turn on a dime

- A compassionate soul who will stand up for those who cannot stand up for themselves

The Queen of Cups
Sun Sign—Cancer
Born Between—22 June and 22 July
Sun Sign Keywords—Emotional, protective, nurturing, kind
Sun Sign Personality Traits

- Internalises and guards their feelings
- Willing to give most things a try

The King of Cups
Sun Sign—Scorpio
Born Between—24 October and 22 November
Sun Sign Keywords—Passionate, extreme, driven, possessive
Sun Sign Personality Traits

- A brooding or mysterious person who oozes temptation
- Someone who holds onto a grudge or perceived wrongdoing for a long time (potentially forever)

THE AIR SIGN FAMILY

The Page of Swords
Can be linked to any of the three air astrological signs: Aquarius, Gemini, Libra. Use the lists of sun sign behaviours and keywords to help you identify which one your page may be.

The Knight of Swords
Sun Sign—Gemini
Born Between—22 May and 21 June
Sun Sign Keywords—Intelligent, adaptable, curious, vicious
Sun Sign Personality Traits

- A person who is very quick to voice their opinion
- A jack of all trades with many arenas of knowledge and interests

The Queen of Swords
Sun Sign—Libra
Born Between—24 September and 23 October

Sun Sign Keywords—Fair, social, charming, self-concerned
Sun Sign Personality Traits

- A natural peacekeeper and negotiator
- Someone who favours being in a relationship more than being on their own

The King of Swords

Sun Sign—Aquarius
Born Between—21 January and 19 February
Sun Sign Keywords—Visionary, inspiring, aloof, detached
Sun Sign Personality Traits

- Will do whatever it takes to be original
- Cares deeply about the future of humanity

If you read the tarot cards with a different set of astrological assignments for the tarot court members, you can transfer the information over to your own set. There is more than one school of thought when it comes to what zodiac sign each of the tarot court members are, and it is better to work with the formula and correspondences that work and make sense for you. It is also best in practice to stick with the astrological assignments that work for you even if you come across external resources that have different information. Take what works for you and apply it to your astrological foundation. Don't throw out something that works just because someone else says something different.

~ Six ~
PREDICTING TIMING
WITH THE TAROT COURT

If you have been reading the tarot for a time this has likely happened to you: you are sitting with your cards, all excited, and you finally get to the card in your tarot spread that is going to tell you "when" and you flip over a court card. Internal screaming ensues. You may have even put the card back in the deck and looked at the next one. No judgement, we have all at least thought about it. Fear not, this is where you learn how to read the court cards in a predictive way once and for all.

There really is quite a scandal in the tarot world when it comes to predictive tarot. It all boils down to each tarot reader's view of whether or not the tarot really can be used to predict the future. Predictive tarot practices and beliefs amongst readers are as varied as we are. Some tarot readers never use the tarot to predict anything, other tarot readers use the tarot to read in a predictive manner exclusively, and some read with a mixed approach, using what comes up in each individual reading. All ways are just as valid.

Predicting outcomes with the tarot can be a tricky practice. Free will makes everything open to change and negotiation. When I read the tarot for my clients, I am often asked about timing, and while I will answer this for them, I also let them know that the tarot does not talk about fixed fates.

For me, the tarot takes a picture and an energetic snapshot of what is going on when the reading is underway. So for my clients I would let them know what the most likely outcome is with respect to timing at the present moment. It is also a wonderful way to allow yourself and the querent a glimpse of the possibilities as there is usually more than once choice or path in front of them. It can show us the path of least resistance, the one where we are likely to find the most challenge, or the one we really should avoid—unless drama and pain are your thing. What road we ultimately walk down, however, is our choice.

There are many tarot readers who believe in destiny and fate. This is usually in varying degrees. Some believe that the big events in our lives are fated, such as whether we are going to have children, but the small things are our own choice. Some tarot readers believe everything is mapped out as a divine plan. If you align with these beliefs, then predicting with the tarot may be easier for you. While I believe professionals in any industry should be cautious of projecting and imposing their religious beliefs on someone when they are working with them, your background and beliefs are going to play a role in how you use the tarot and how you believe it works when it comes to prediction.

If using the tarot for prediction is something that makes you break out into a cold sweat, then don't use this in your practice. There are plenty of amazing tarot readers who do not use the tarot in a predictive sense at all. Don't force yourself. If this is the case and you don't want to read timing questions, then make sure you let your future clients know. Have a space on your website where you let people know what kind of reading you are going to be giving them and what you will not predict. The right people will find you and you don't want to do something that makes you feel reluctant to pick up your tarot deck in the first place.

When it comes to prediction, there is an added element of considering when it comes to long term predictions. While you are defining your predictive tarot guidelines, predicting long-term events is something I recommend that you have outlined for yourself. If you feel comfortable carrying out readings where you are asking the tarot to look years ahead, then go for it.

My professional practice is to only carry out readings within a twelve month period. A lot can change for a person and their situation within twelve months. It has always been my belief that you only do what feels right for you.

THE COURT TELLS US WHEN

If you are looking to use the tarot as a predictive tool, here are some techniques that you can use to help find out the timing of your tarot readings for our beloved court cards.

Keep things as simple as possible when it comes to timing. I highly recommend giving your court cards associations and clear timing definitions. You don't need to bury yourself under yet another layer of the tarot. Timing for me is a clear and quick answer that should require little elaboraton.

These are popular timing associations for the suit elements that you can use in your practice. If you read or own a tarot deck that uses different ones, please go with what works for you.

The Seasons
- Wands—Summer
- Swords—Autumn
- Cups—Spring
- Pentacles—Winter

The Court Cards
- Pages—Days
- Knights—Weeks
- Queens—Months
- Kings—Years

TIMING WITH THE WANDS COURT

Page of Wands indicates days in summer. If you carry out the reading during the summer months, then this would indicate sudden change or within days. If you carry out the reading outside of the summer months, it would indicate that the reading outcome will manifest within the first few days of the next summer.

Knight of Wands indicates weeks in summer. If you carry out the reading during the summer months, then this would indicate change within a week or two. If you carry out the reading outside of the summer months, it would indicate that the reading outcome will manifest within the first week of the next summer.

Queen of Wands indicates months in summer. If you carry out the reading while in the summer months, then this would indicate change will take place within one of those months. If you carry out the reading at another time, it would indicate that the reading outcome will manifest within the next summer months.

King of Wands indicates years in summer, with this being a longer reach for prediction. I recommend that you wait at least six months or until something major has changed and then ask the question again.

TIMING WITH THE PENTACLES COURT

Page of Pentacles indicates days in winter. If you carry out the reading during the winter months, then this would indicate sudden change or within days. If you carry out the reading outside of the winter months, it would indicate that the reading outcome will manifest within the first few days of the next winter.

Knight of Pentacles indicates weeks in winter, so if you carry out the reading during winter, then this would indicate change within a week or two. If you carry out the reading while out of the winter months, it would indicate that the reading outcome will manifest within the first week of the next winter.

Queen of Pentacles indicates months in winter. If you carry out the reading while in the winter months, then this would indicate change will take place within one of those months. If you carry out the reading outside of the winter months, it would indicate that the reading outcome will manifest within the next coming winter months.

King of Pentacles indicates years in winter. With this being a longer reach for prediction, I recommend that you wait at least six months or until something major has changed and then ask the question again.

TIMING WITH THE SWORDS COURT

Page of Swords indicates days in autumn. If you carry out the reading during the autumn months, this would indicate sudden change or within days. If you carry out the reading outside of the autumn months, it would indicate that the reading outcome will manifest within the first few days of the next autumn.

Knight of Swords indicates weeks in autumn. If you carry out the reading while in the autumn months, this would indicate change within a week or two. If you carry out the reading outside of the autumn months, it would indicate that the reading outcome will manifest within the first week of the next autumn.

Queen of Swords indicates months in autumn so if you carry out the reading during the autumn months, this would indicate change will take place within one of those months. If you carry out the reading while out of the autumn months, it would indicate that the reading outcome will manifest within the next coming autumn months.

King of Swords indicates years in autumn, with this being a longer reach for prediction. I recommend that you wait at least six months or until something major has changed and then ask the question again.

TIMING WITH THE CUPS COURT

Page of Cups indicates days in spring. If you carry out the reading during the spring months, then this would indicate sudden change or within days. If you carry out the reading outside of the spring months, it would indicate that the reading outcome will manifest within the first few days of the next spring.

Knight of Cups indicates weeks in spring, so if you carry out the reading during the spring months, this would indicate change within a week or two. If you carry out the reading outside of the spring months, it would indicate that the reading outcome will manifest within the first week of the next spring.

Queen of Cups indicates months in spring. If you carry out the reading while in the spring months, then this would indicate change will take place within one of those months. If you carry out the reading while out of the spring months, it would indicate that the reading outcome will manifest within the next coming spring months.

King of Cups indicates years in spring, with this being a longer reach for prediction. I recommend that you wait at least six months or until something major has changed and then ask the question again.

EXERCISE: YOUR PERSONAL COURT

This exercise is a great way to do some creative profiling of real people. By carrying out this exercise, you will be able to link real life people, via their behaviours and characteristics, to the tarot court cards. It is easiest if you use the people you know well in your life for this exercise, like your family and friends. You can also use your work colleagues and/or archnemesis if you want to choose some other people for this exercise. You will be putting the information you have learned so far in this book to work.

You will need a full set of the tarot court (all sixteen cards), a notebook, and pen for this practicum.

1. Create a list of people you know.

2. Collect their date of birth information. At the very least you will need their day and month of birth.

3. Write down which court card they are using the zodiac table information in chapter 5

4. Take a big picture and look at the people with whom you surround yourself. Are they all knights? (I bet if they are, there is always some drama and action going on.) Have an abundance of pentacles people who like their security and routine more than risk? Too many pages? Maybe it is time for some grown-up friends (although they can be overrated at times too).

5. Now take another look at the list. Is there an abundance of one family of court cards? Do you have a lot of wand court cards in your life or does another element dominate your social circles? How do you believe this affects your interactions? Or are there any odd people out?

6. How does this information help you understand the people in your life and the relationships you have with them?

It is always an interesting experience exploring and discovering the people we share our lives with, as it can often be a reflection of ourselves. You can use the questions offered here in the exercise to reflect and journal or to expand your knowledge of the court cards.

~ Seven ~
HIERARCHY, ROLES, AND THE PROGRESSION OF THE TAROT COURT

Hierarchy as a system can be problematic when it comes to a spiritual tool like the tarot, as it can seem as rigid and outdated as the court itself. While many Western mystery schools, churches, and organisations still revolve around a system of rank and importance, many tarot professionals and students are more rebellious at heart and don't want to be labeled or numbered. The court, however, is a system and does have a built-in hierarchy. So how can we interpret and integrate that for modern tarot readers?

The rank of the tarot court starts at the pages, who are the servants of the court, and ends at the most "powerful" person, the king. Because the tarot was born from a playing card game, this makes sense, as this is the based on the structure of a pack of playing cards.

Instead of seeing the hierarchy as something that increases or lessens someone's value, power, and influence, we are going to explore how this can change the person's strengths and roles, instead, by giving each tarot court member value in their position in the court. Just because someone doesn't have a crown does not mean you should underestimate them.

With all of this in mind, we are now going to explore the roles of each of the tarot court members along with some of their associations and how they come into play.

THE PAGES—COMMUNICATING

Pages were traditionally lower level servants to the court whose duties to the other members have changed over time. It was seen that the next step in a page's life (often seen in most tarot decks as young males) was to train as a squire and then one day become a knight. As a page, they were in the entry point to the noble class.

As a collective group, they are full of potential. They want adventure, action, to be included and heard, and to make an impact. They may also be impatient and lack the means to have the impact that they want in the world. Pages are also very easy to influence, so there is much power in being a mentor to a page.

Pages were not only responsible for taking care of daily tasks for others; they were also messengers, and this is where their connection to communication comes into play. There is a lot of power in being the one who carries information to and fro. Just think of the things that someone in that position could overhear, interpret, pass on to certain people, and distort.

Some key words for all pages:
- To be of service
- Messenger
- Runs the messages (is the carrier not the keeper)
- Gopher
- Can indicate children or pregnancy
- Immature
- Simple
- Reactive
- Without a lot of independence

In a Reading

When a page is presented in a position in a tarot spread that is aligned to a solution, next step, or the future, look to how you are or are not communicating. Take this a step further with the elemental alignment of the page that is present. Communication from the heart (cups), logical communication (swords), practical communication (pentacles) or argumentative, willed communication (wands). Whatever suit the page belongs to or what cards are surrounding the page in that reading, communication is the key to moving forward and it cannot be overlooked.

Page of Cups

Mantra—"I feel"

Just because feelings are the key to the suit doesn't always mean that the message is eloquent. Being young in nature, the page's message may come in a variety of ways. (Being on the coast of the ocean, the weather can change quickly from flat calm seas to tsunamis and wild storms; this often volatile change can be seen in the mood swings of a Page of Cups.) The Page of Cups child is very emotional, feeling everything in extremes and tends to be extremely empathic. If you are around a Page of Cups child or have one of your own, it may be an idea to teach them as early as you can how to cleanse and protect their own energy fields. My mother ensured that I wore an amethyst crystal at all times when I was going through a very rough patch as a child and it helped immensely.

The Page of Cups may indicate a new child in the family or that of a close friend. Of all of the pages, this one has meant new babies more than any other in my tarot practice.

In a Reading

Meanings—Emotional news coming soon, dreams coming true, expression of base emotions, pregnancy or a new baby

For Reflection—Are you listening to children around you?

This could easily have been about your own emotions, and I encourage people to tune in to their emotions and their emotional bodies, but I challenge you to take this a step further. Are you listening to the children in your life? If you don't have any of your own, look at spending some time with your family or get in touch with your inner child. Children have the most amazing way of viewing the world and they will often pull no punches. Experience life as a child once in awhile. You may be amazed at what transpires for you.

Page of Pentacles

Mantra—"I do"

The Page of Pentacles is the type of child (if it is a child) who is constantly in need of a bath, as they have spent all day up a tree, in the mud, and playing with animals. These pages form deep connections to animals and nature. They are always doing something with their hands. Page of Pentacles children tend to be a quieter bunch that would rather create and figure things out by pulling things apart and seeing for themselves than asking how something works. Some people may have the tendency to want to rush this type of child along because they tend to do things in their own time, but this is just who they are: grounded and very practical. They want to be the ones who tie their own shoes and buckle themselves in the car. They also make laundry day fun.

In a Reading

Meanings—Financial news coming soon, creating new things, building, expression of base physical needs and wants

For Reflection—Are you listening to what your body is telling you?

Sometimes it can be a physical reaction to a food we eat or your body wanting exercise. If you have the Page of Pentacles in a reading, this could be something for you to consider.

Page of Swords

Mantra—"I ask"

The Page of Swords child constantly asks questions. "Why" is their favourite word and, as my mother said about me as a child, "Teaching her how to talk wasn't the trick—it was teaching her to be quiet." To note, this is a good example of how people exemplify the archetypes—as you read earlier, I was a Page of Cups child, but I was also a Page of Swords. It is common for people to be more than one archetype, especially in different areas of their life (social/emotional/etc.)

A Page of Swords tends to be drawn to anything to do with language. They sing all the time even if they don't know the right words. And they talk, sometimes to themselves or the spirits that others can't see. They are the type of child that is told repeatedly to be quiet and go to sleep. They are observant, will offer the solution to problems, and want to help with their keen minds. Frustration can mount when they are overlooked due to their age.

In a Reading

Meanings—Inspiring news coming soon, understanding and inspiration coming to you, words that you don't actually mean falling from your mouth, clear communication required

For Reflection—Are you listening to what you are saying?

This may seem pretty basic, but it is surprising just how many people have no idea of what they are saying and what they are telling themselves. Thoughts are things. Words have energy and what you spend the majority of your time telling others and yourself affects your life. So take some time to be conscious of the words and thoughts that you project. Be kind to yourself, and if you are in a place where this is hard, then a simple mantra like "I am loved" can do you the world of good.

Page of Wands

Mantra—"I create"

The Page of Wands is aligned with fire. It doesn't mean they are going to run around burning things. If this is happening, probably best to dig a little deeper as to why and lock away the lighters. The Page of Wands child will, however, like all things bright and shiny. They also tend to be super excitable and full of energy. They love to run, skip, skate, and do everything as actively as possible. These bundles of energy simply cannot sit still. If you have or are with children of fire, then the more physical activity you can expose them to, the better. Creative endeavours come as natural as breathing to the Page of Wands child, which is another exceptional outlet for their energy.

In a Reading

Meanings—New creative endeavours, messages of change, activity and adventure

For Reflection—Are you listening to what your spirit is telling you?

If you are feeling down in the dumps or as if inspiration is lacking, this card can be the messenger saying that it is time to start energising your spirit. Ways to do that include exercise, meditation, yoga, and (my favourite way) having some fun. The soul loves it when we are having fun. Our inner child (which is perfect for the page cards) is delighted by laughter and joy. Do something that you love to do. Every week if you can, even better if it is every day.

THE KNIGHTS—DARING

To become a knight, you have to be given the title and knighted by a member of a monarchy. Knights were often given power in a number of ways. They were trusted to be protectors of their lords and ladies, collected taxes on behalf of the monarchy, and most famously, were given power in military capacity. Knights were not always seen as nobility. This happened during the late Middle Ages, and their codes and legends evolved throughout history. There are even knights today, although the title is an honorary one.

This is where the knights in the tarot derive their key meaning from. Every knight in the tarot takes action. They all have their own code and ideals and do things in their own way, but they all act on behalf of something.

They are the extended arm of the ruling power able to do the things that kings and queens, mantled with responsibilities, cannot. Knights are often associated with fighting and were highly valued if they were skilled warriors. Most famous writings about knights are written about these warrior men.

In the Rider-Waite Smith Tarot, we see them depicted in a very European way, astride horses. Even the body language of the horses in the deck can give you important clues as to the meaning of the card and personality of each of the knights.

Key words for all of the knights

- Action
- Idealistic

- Self-centered
- Purpose driven
- Quests
- Of service to the kingdom
- Valour
- Camelot
- Romance
- Strength
- Courage
- Dedication and training
- Code of conduct
- Warrior
- Self-sacrificing
- Groups
- Modes of transport (seen on horses in many tarot decks)
- Romantic

In a Reading

When a knight is presented in a position in a tarot spread that is aligned to a solution, next step, or the future, look to taking action, moving forward, and using that knights' energy to dare to do so. Take this a step further with the elemental alignment of the knight that is present. Acting from the heart (cups), finally putting your inspiration to paper and acting on your ideas (swords), acting on behalf of your body (pentalces)—which can be as simple as going to the gym or getting that check-up at the doctor's that you have been putting off—or spiritual exploration or taking steps to get your dream job (wands).

Whatever suit the knight belongs to or what cards are surrounding the knight, the time to take action is near. No more being on the sidelines of your own life. Knights also act on behalf of the greater good and their community so take that into consideration as well. Every action has an impact on the people around it, whether we see it or not.

The Knight of Cups

Mantra—"Love is the highest power"

This knight is extremely passionate and does everything for love: love of their monarch, love of their role in life and love of a higher power—even love for another person. Their loyalty and devotion comes from the heart. They can be extremely hot headed when they are crossed or betrayed. Their code revolves around the ideal that love is the highest power and will openly disagree with anyone who fights for anything less. They will be forever searching for the perfect love and are more concerned with the vision and capture of this love than actually keeping it. Someone new on the horizon will take their fancy and off they go again.

In a Reading

Meanings—A new lover, or even an old lover returning, working on the things that you love, acting out of love, heart-centred choices, protecting the things you love, always searching for love, a romantic date or getaway

For Reflection—How often do you act out of love?

This can be for a person that you love or even out of love of something. How does this feel when you do this? Is it easy for you to act from a space of love? Don't forget to take action when it comes to self-love too. It's just as important as acting on behalf of someone else, if not more so.

The Knight of Pentacles

Mantra—"I endure all in service"

This knight will be there after everyone else has given up. They seem to have an almost superhuman source of perseverance when they are carrying out their purpose. While this knight is slower to make decisions, once they are made they are unwavering in their resolve. They are the most loyal friend that you could ever ask for and will make sure that the goal is reached no matter what lays ahead. They know that even one small step forward is progress. This knight will also be the one who makes sure that everyone's horses are well watered and fed and that there is enough wood for the campfire at night.

In a Reading

Meanings—Longterm decisions and actions that have long-reaching implications, loyalty, preparation for the road ahead, slow and steady progress, not giving up, a loyal person in your life, acting out of loyalty

For Reflection—Where is your loyalty?

When you dig deep, what are you really doing? Where are your motivations and alliances? This is especially good to work on if you feel like you have gone off the trail of your purpose in life.

The Knight of Swords

Mantra—"I know what to do"

You do not want to get in this knight's way as you are likely to get run down by their horse. It is also highly recommended that you don't start an argument with this knight. They will shut you down or shut you up. This knight has high intellectual ideals and they tend to suffer fools very ungraciously. They can often seem aloof and lost in thought as they rarely stop thinking and can have trouble shutting their minds down. This knight is a person you want to listen to in regards to tactics and strategy as they are often two steps ahead of even the most intelligent of enemies.

In a Reading

Meanings—Wisdom in actions, sudden inspiration, knowledge is power, use what you know, don't just sit on it, act now, especially if you have been dwelling on things for far too long, take action as soon as clarity is achieved

For Reflection—Are you thinking before you act?

Even when you feel that the path forward is extremely clear, it is a good idea to think carefully before you act. There may be other perspectives to consider before you go all guns blazing into unknown territory.

The Knight of Wands

Mantra—"I will clear the path"

This knight is always ready for an adventure and loves nothing more than to discover something or someone new. They are always itching for a fight and are likely to start one if there hasn't been a conflict recently. While they are restless, they are excellent allies when you need someone to protect and fight for you. This knight will charge ahead and clear your way of any danger and will not hesitate to carry out orders.

In a Reading

Meanings—Travel and adventure, new experiences and new people coming into your life, standing up for yourself, boundaries getting pushed, being hot headed about something, getting out of a situation that is tying you down, an ally who is going to fight for you.

For Reflection—What kind of adventure are you seeking?

We all have different ideas of what constitutes an adventure. By working with the energy of this knight, you are being challenged to go outside your comfort zone. Seeking out new experiences and pushing your boundaries can unlock hidden talents and unleash more of your personal potential. Even better, if there is a sale on for your favourite holiday destination, book that ticket.

THE QUEENS—NURTURING

A queen is defined as a woman of authority. Traditionally queens had a very different pathway to power and leadership than their male counterparts. In many countries women weren't allowed to rule like men and often women were traded for political gains and alliances. This can be seen as the queen having to marry or be given her power by someone else. While this may certainly be true depending on the situation, when a queen comes up in a reading, times have changed. Arranged marriages still happen, women and men still marry for money, social status and power. So while it may seem archaic to reference one of the traditional ways queens came into power, it is still relevant. Queens can also be born into their role and can lead countries just as well as kings can. They just tend to lead in a different way.

The queens are leaders. They are change makers and they hold huge amounts of influence. They are often more admired than kings because of their more approachable nature in the tarot court. It would be wise not to let this approachability fool you. The queens are not to be underestimated in any way.

Key words for all queens:
- Motherhood
- Teacher
- Manipulative
- High Maintenance
- Passive power
- Runs the castle (remember we can ALL be the queens no matter the gender identification of a person)
- Luxurious
- Creative
- Emotional

In a Reading
When a queen is presented in a position in a tarot spread that is aligned to a solution, next step, or the future, look at what needs nurturing in the situation. Take this a step further with the elemental alignment of the queen that is present, as that will likely tell you what is in desperate need of some TLC. Self-care, forgiveness and self-love and also caring for those you love (cups), study, nurturing the mind, nurturing ideals and being inspired (swords) nurturing the body, taking care of a garden or living space and the home (pentacles) nurturing your ambition, further education for your career, mentoring, your spiritual side, (wands). Whatever suit the queen belongs to or what cards are surrounding the queen in that reading, growth and care is the key to moving forward and it cannot be overlooked.

The Queen of Cups
Mantra—"I nurture though love and emotions"
This queen is the walking personification of the moon. She is ever-changing but brings stability and knowledge with her life experience to station. Her intuition is incredibly accurate and she is in-tune with her emotions and her

emotional needs. She is reflective, nurturing and will put the needs of others above her own She knows all things are connected and feels that very deeply. She will nurture her relationships and believes that love is the way to solve most problems.

In a Reading

Meanings—Healing emotionally, emotional maturity, being in touch with your feelings, making decisions based on emotions alone, being emotionally over the top, emotionally manipulating or being manipulated.

For Reflection—When was the last time you honoured your feelings?

We often know what we need to do in certain situations, but embodying this can be hard. This reflective prompt is inviting you to put your emotional needs first. If something does not feel right, trust your inner compass and yourself by saying no and avoiding future pain.

The Queen of Pentacles

Mantra—"I nurture through the body"

The Queen of Pentacles is all about her home and hearth and her children. Don't think just because you aren't a blood child of this queen that it will matter. If you are sick, the Queen of Pentacles will be there with soup and an herbal remedy to take care of you. If you are having relationship problems, the Queen of Pentacles will put on the kettle and feed your soul while you talk about your love life. This is the Queen of Pentacles. Come into her home and she will take you in and nurture you as one of her own. You will often find a Queen of Pentacles in her garden or in her kitchen.

In a Reading

Meanings—Time to get back to your roots, nurturing through home and hearth, level headedness, practical guidance and practical love, being in your body, healing the body

For Reflection—Are you physically taking care of yourself?

You may have grand plans to scale Mt. Everest, but if you do not take care of your body, you may as well forget it. Another interesting reflective exercise with this queen is to see how your body reacts to being mothered in this way. Does it trigger you? Why?

The Queen of Swords

Mantra—*"I nurture through the mind"*

The Queen of Swords is fair and intelligent and can see through BS a mile away. People will come to her to learn and to seek out fair judgement or solutions. She will answer your question with a question, leading you to your own conclusions and revelations rather than just tell you the answer. Her words are her weapons and she knows how to use them well. Nothing cuts like the words from an enraged Queen of Swords. This queen can be seen as cold and calculating or guarded. Knowledge is the way she wants to heal and nurture herself and others.

In a Reading

Meanings—Viewing things from an unbiased perspective, truth over sentiment, getting clarity, being careful of the words you use

For Reflection—Are you asking the right questions?

The answers are there; you just have to ask the right questions. It is not the time to beat around the bush. If you want something, ask for it clearly and directly. Furthermore, are you asking the right people or too many people for the answers?

The Queen of Wands

Mantra—*"I nurture through the soul"*

This queen shines brightly and cannot help but have people drawn to her light. She is the reminder to live a life that we are passionate about. Her journey is through experience, self-expression, and determination. You will often find this queen either doing something creative and expressive or surrounded by people. No matter what she does, she will do it with all of her being and this is incredibly attractive to the people around her.

In a Reading

Meanings—Going after your goals, being inspired, or being an inspiration to others, spiritual healing, self-care, dynamic energy, enthusiastic, clear self-expression

For Reflection—Are you going after what you really want?

This queen is the perfect energy to work with if you are finding it hard to live the life that you truly desire. This is a perfect energy to work with if you have any fear around living authentically, as it will be burned away through acts of self-expression. She is the queen of living an authentic life.

THE KINGS—LEADING

Historically speaking, not just anyone could be a king, kings weren't made, they were born into a wealthy, noble family. This can be said of all of the members of the royal court. This is something to keep in mind when any court card comes up in a reading. This can mean that when a king appears in a tarot reading and it represents the querent that they are naturally aligned to within the realm of leadership, they are born to do it.

Kings had responsibility thrust upon them at birth. They could only abdicate if they had someone to pass that responsibility on to and historically speaking, not a lot of people volunteered to step down. Most people would kill to be king and many people did.

Leadership comes at a cost. All eyes are on the one who rules. Actions and decisions can create wars or treaties, and there are always people who are going to question the person in charge. So the king asks, "Do you really want to rule?" It is a heavy responsibility, a duty to others. People are often aware that there would be those who would love to see them fail, but they continue on and their motivating factors can be found in their elemental associations.

When the kings come up in a reading, you can look to other cards to see if the king is ruling for the benefit of others or selfishly; if they are unbalanced in their approach and view in life. Do they rule the kingdom blindly or indifferently to the impact they are making, or are they in touch with the world?

Another aspect of the kings is that they do not really have to answer to anyone and their word is final. When this is challenged, each king is going to react in a different way. Kings are used to getting their own way and may not appreciate people challenging them, especially in public.

Key words for all of the kings
- Ruler
- Maturity
- Strength
- Serious
- Image to uphold
- Ruthless
- Selfless
- Macrocosmic (keeps the bigger picture in mind)
- Authority
- Leader
- Dominance
- Statistician
- Planning
- Responsibility

In a Reading
When a king is presented in a position in a tarot spread that is aligned to a solution, next step, or the future, look at all aspects of leadership. Where is the leadership? Are people defecting to you to lead them or are you giving your power away? Take this a step further with the elemental alignment of the king that is present. Leading from a place of love (cups), leading with the larger community in mind, intelligent leadership (swords), down to earth leadership and physically being there for people in the position of leader

(pentacles), or building something from scratch and then leading in a new way (wands)? Whatever suit the king belongs to or what cards are surrounding the king in that reading, leadership is the key to moving forward and it cannot be overlooked.

The King of Cups

Mantra—"I lead with my heart"

The King of Cups will put their family first, which includes people who they consider family and the people who are under their care. The well-being of their kingdom and their people is always at the forefront of their minds. They have to feel good about their position of leadership and with the people that they deal with. This king is very good at calming potential conflicts and is a wonderful diplomat.

In a Reading

Meanings—Lead through love, make compassionate decisions, self-love and self-care as a practice of importance, diplomacy, trusting your intuition about the people in your life and that you work with

For Reflection—Do you engage your heart when making choices?

Working with this king will connect your mind and your heart, allowing for the choices that you make to be in alignment with your feelings. Being the compassionate leader that the King of Cups is, this card challenges you to look at how your decisions are affecting others.

The King of Pentacles

Mantra—"I lead with my wallet"

The King of Pentacles will ensure that every penny and cent is accounted for. They are masters at business and money and want to know what the return on investment is going to be in every undertaking of their life. Natural resources are extremely important to them and so is their standard of living. They like practical approaches to leading and making decisions, and are less likely to be swayed than the rest of the tarot court.

In a Reading

Meanings—Money is power, making smart choices with your resources, ensuring you have enough to take care of yourself, living within your means, taking care of business, practical steps forward, well worn paths

For Reflection—Are you trying to reinvent the wheel for no reason?

Change is good, but sometimes we want to change things for no good reason. This king is excellent to work with if you are resisting doing the work you need to do. Remember the return on your investment is going to make the work worth it.

The King of Swords

Mantra—"I lead with logic"

The King of Swords can be one scary MF. They are extremely intelligent and have no problems using their intellect to get what they want. They are adept at finding loopholes when they need one and will talk their way out of any situation. They have laser focus and will not be manipulated easily. This king will surround themselves with the brightest minds and if they are a good leader, will know where their weaknesses lie and ensure that they are covered in that area too. They will make logical decisions for the people that are under their care.

In a Reading

Meanings—Use your words carefully and get to the point, look at things from every angle possible before moving forward, cover your blind spots well, look at the big picture, making smart choices

For Reflection—What is the smartest way forward from here?

This king is connected to vision and the ability to connect with possible futures. They live in the world of possibilities and are wonderful to work with when it comes to finding clarity.

The King of Wands

Mantra—"I lead with passion"

The King of Wands draws people to them, as their passion for what they believe in is infectious. When people are around the King of Wands they feel as though they are being ignited, whether this is something long term or not, it is a powerful exchange. They make decisions often through their beliefs and are dedicated to their vision. They respond well to people who are also passionate about the same things. The King of Wands is a passionate partner and ally and is quick to have your back if you are in their good books.

In a Reading

Meanings—Inspiring others, reigning in your impulses, applying power wisely, standing firmly by what you believe in, charismatic personalities, being bold

For Reflection—Are you working on your passions?

Carving out time to work on what we truly love is incredibly important. Working with the bold King of Wands can help you make decisions that lead you to your passions.

~ Eight ~
ARCHETYPES AND THE TAROT COURT

So what exactly is an archetype and why give the tarot court archetypal dignitaries in the first place? An archetype is essentially seen as a "typical example" of something or an original that has been copied and imitated over and over but remains, in essence, the same. They are connecting themes, representations, stereotypes, and embodiments that are cross-sectional throughout culture and geographic location.

In Jungian psychology, archetypes are popular and well-known. They are used widely in the metaphysical and New Age community. Jung coined the term "collective unconscious," which is our humanity's hive mind. It is the collection of the symbols, mythologies, instincts, and archetypes that we all share. This is why we will find that in many cultures around the world there is always a goddess of love or a god or war. These are perfect examples of cross-sectional archetypes, as love and fighting are common no matter where you come from. Humanity has collective experiences that give us common ground.

Why are they so important and useful in the context of the tarot? The seventy-eight tarot cards themselves can be seen as visual representations of archetypes: common experiences, relationships, figures, and people in your life.

This is one of the reasons that the tarot is so popular around the world. We see ourselves and our loved ones in the cards. We recognise our experiences, shared pain and triumphs, and even the people we loathe in a pack of cards.

Each of the tarot court members has their own archetype on top of their title. This is a way to understand the cards and what they mean in a reading. They are also a wonderful way to explore the tarot court as a personal development tool and a way to understand aspects of ourselves. As with all personal explorations, we can then see how these archetypes interact with others and point out the way we are in certain relationship dynamics.

Here are offerings of the tarot court as seen as universal archetypes. We are going to dive deep into these archetypes of the tarot court. Allowing the members of the court to have a recognisable energy removes any confusion around who they are in a reading because of their actions, reactions, and behaviours. These are my offerings to you as archetypes. You may find that you don't agree with them. That's OK. Take what works for you and leave the rest. I have used the tarot court cards traditional titles as well as the archetype titles interchangeably in this section for ease.

While exploring the tarot archetypes, remember you can be any of the archetypes presented, no matter the title or the assigned gender that the title or deck you are working with has alloted the court card. It is all about the characteristics and behaviours, not about the sexy bits you may have.

THE KING OF CUPS

Keywords:

- Family orientated
- Sexual
- Thoughtful
- Connected
- Transformative
- Charismatic
- Deep

Astrology—Scorpio

The King of Cups is the lord of the eighth house of astrology. This is the house of sex, death, inheritance, power, transformation, and psychology. This house is the most polarising house due to the taboo nature of some of its key themes. People may have extreme reactions to things like death, power, and sex.

Bad Bitches Tarot and Tarot Mucha

Archetype—Hades—Lord of the Subconscious/Underworld

The King of Cups as Hades takes on the role as the Dark Lord but not in a negative way. They are just comfortable with things that make most people very uncomfortable. They are aware of their dark side and have embraced it. A true King of Cups in their power has gone through the dark night of the soul and has incorporated it into their psyche. This completeness in their power can mean that they are very intimidating or too intense for some people, primarily those who are afraid of their own dark sides.

If the King of Cups is in their shadow, they may be an overly emotional person who tends to deal with their emotions in unhealthy ways, whether that is excessive drinking, cheating, or violence. The King of Cups does nothing by halves; they are all in, for better or worse. On the other side of this extreme, the King of Cups can also totally withdraw, shutting down emotionally—brooding for long periods of time until they are good and ready to deal with their stuff. No one is going to force them to come out of their gothic mood.

The King of Cups can often get lost in their own emotions. They will think things through before making decisions and are very careful about who they let influence them. They aren't into sharing their tactics, preferring to keep their cards close to their chest. Showing weaknesses or opportunities for failure is not something they tend to handle well.

The King of Cups/Hades has a deep sense of loyalty. They live by their own personal code and tend to put family first. They are the kind of leader who wants their children to take the reigns of their legacy and keep it alive. They do not want to write their children's destiny for them, although in some cases they just might, because they have spent a lot of time and energy building their legacy and they feel that this is the right path for them to take.

In Love and Relationships

The King of Cups is very intense and only wants to be with someone where there is a deep connection, sexually and emotionally. If you are shallow and care more about what is happening on your favourite reality TV show than what is going on in the world, then you may get one hell of a steamy night in the bedroom with this lover, but they ain't sticking around. They are well known for being quite the lover and people who are with a King of Cups will have fun trying to keep up with them in the bedroom. The King of Cups falls deeply and completely in love. They adore their family and will put their welfare first when making decisions.

People often swarm to Hades intensity, but many can't handle it. The King of Cups is known to be very honest and may at times be too forthright, bordering on cruel. This is usually not their intention. It is just that small talk and niceties are not always their strong suit, and they would rather cut the crap and get to the heart of the matter. The words that they hear also affect them deeply, don't let that confident exterior fool you; they care what people think of then, especially if they are into you.

The King of Cups is very generous, compassionate, and cultured. They carefully choose who they spend their time with. If you are one of the chosen ones, count yourself very lucky because they will shower you with their love. Once betrayed, the King of Cups will never have the same relationship with you, even if the betrayal is forgiven. They will not forget and there is very little chance of a romantic relationship working with the King of Cups once there has been infidelity. They will more than likely just cut you out of their lives and never look back. You have been warned.

If acting from their shadow, The King of Cups can manipulate situations without anyone ever knowing it happened. They sense what peoples' motivations are and can use that to their advantage. They are also not above a little blackmail, or a lot, depending on just how badly they want what you have. In the extreme, the King of Cups can become codependent in a relationship or even abusive if they have not healed from their own past trauma.

At Work and Career

The King of Cups is drawn to any position where they can influence people. They will seek positions like ministers and religious leaders, motivational speakers, and sales people. These roles are natural selections for the King of Cups. They are also drawn to the ocean and bodies of water, so jobs such as sailors, fisherman, surfers, and marine biologists also suit them. Because death, change, and transition are also parts of this archetype, they will be drawn to working in the field of medicine, nursing, psychology, and death rights.

Hades is a passionate leader. If they believe in the work that they are doing, they will do just about anything for their team and the people who help them achieve their goals. As a manager the King of Cups honours loyalty and truth and wants to work with people who are not afraid to shake things up.

If the King of Cups is working in their shadow, they can be a bit of a conman who uses their sexuality to get what they want and doesn't want to actually work for anything. Why do something when you can sleep your way to the top and get everyone else to work for you?

Indicators that you are a King of Cups/Hades archetype

- You desire a deep emotional connection in your relationships. It is all or nothing.
- Seduction is one of your strengths and people often refer to you as charming.
- You have been through trauma in your life and not only survived but thrived.
- You can naturally sense other peoples' dark sides and are drawn to peoples' shadow selves.
- You are highly intuitive.
- Power and sex for you are often connected.

King of Cups Strengths

- Aware of their power and affect on people
- Wise and perceptive
- Cultured
- Fearless
- Excellent in tense and difficult situations
- Creative

King of Cups Shadow Side

- Manipulative
- Dark/moody/broody
- Prone to addictions
- Destructive
- Projects emotions if it gets too intense
- Arrogant

The King of Cups Archetype in a Tarot Reading

Identifying the tarot court as either an aspect of yourself playing out or another person is something that can trip up even the most experienced tarot

reader. When the King of Cups comes up in a tarot reading, be on the look-out for these behaviours as identifiers:

- Motivation—A person who is acting out of loyalty and protection of the people that they love and who they consider family.

- Observing highly emotional and intense situations without taking it personally or letting negativity affect you.

- A person who is quieter, highly attractive, and has a dangerous and tempting sexy aura. The person that you know is going to be trouble but you just can't help yourself.

If the King of Cups comes up in a position that requires an outcome, action, or the next step forward, consider these actions as suggestions to move into the archetype's power:

- Ask yourself—How can I handle this situation or tackle this obstacle with more emotional maturity and peace?

- Journey into self-exploration, work with understanding your strengths and limits, and develop your surroundings to support those things.

- Consider other peoples' feelings and motivations in the situation and how it can be affecting the people involved and the situation itself.

- Ask—What would Hades do? Work with the mythology of the archetype to gain in-depth answers and options for moving forward. As with many myths, they can be intense, especially when it comes to Hades, so don't take things too literally.

The Queen of Cups

Keywords

- Sensitive
- Open
- Intuitive
- Loving
- Spiritual
- Psychic
- Mysterious

Everyday Witch Tarot and Steampunk Tarot

Astrology—Cancer

The Queen of Cups holds dominion over the fourth house of astrology, which is the house of home and family. It is the space of parents, children, relations, and the deep needs that we have connected to home and family.

Archetype—The Mystic—The Priestess and the Psychic

The Queen of Cups as the Mystic is deep, emotional, psychic, spiritual, and naturally healing. They know things innately and are very connected to their intuition and emotions. They know that there is deep power in them and will honor their gifts and use them to help others. The Mystic is gifted at opening others to their natural intuitive and psychic abilities and is often drawn to spiritual paths that support their skills from a very early age.

This is the archetype that will know what someone is going to say before they do and can feel the vibe in a room just by entering it. They often dream vividly and seem to be a little aloof compared to more down to earth archetypes, because they always have one foot (or even half of their bodies) in the spiritual and energetic realm. They will be drawn to crystals, earth spirits (like faeries), and magical items of all kinds and will take to tools such as the tarot with grace and ease.

The Queen of Cups is also nurturing, sensitive, and caring. They are the type of person who loves, cares, and emotionally supports all children, whether they are biologically linked or not. They know that children are important and need care from us to change the world, and sees the future potential in many of the people that they cares for, they see the potential in all people. This is an extension of their psychic abilities, and in this way, they are being of service to spirit by supporting those around them.

The Mystic can be overprotective and overwhelming if they have not done any spiritual work themselves or if they let their emotions rule them when it comes to their expression in the world. They are not afraid to use tears to get what they want and they are the masters of emotional manipulation and guilting people. You won't even realise that you are being triggered to respond the way they want you to.

If the Mystic acts out of their shadow, they will be ruthless and cold and won't bat an eyelid when it comes to using what they know about people against them. They can also attract extremely ugly energies to their side, and if they lack a conscience, they will be very good at scamming people out of their hard earned cash.

In Love and Relationships

The Queen of Cups is a devoted and warm partner. They live for their partner and family. They love being around the people they adore and who adore them and are deeply romantic. Being a natural caretaker, they can assume that role in a relationship and can be attracted to people who need healing or taking care of. They also tend to know the people that they are in relationships with better than they know themselves. This can backfire on the Mystic as they seem to fall in love with the untapped potential of their partner and not the reality. Because they can see what could be and not always what is, they stick around for longer than they should.

They can slip into codependency very easily, especially if they have had issues with worthiness or have had partners belittle their intuitive gifts. If their need to be loved outweighs their need to be who they truly are, they will gravitate toward and choose a partner who will deny their intuitive gifts and oppress their true nature, forcing their gifts and talents away for the sake of acceptance.

The Queen of Cups can also tend to disappear into the background of a relationship. They do not overly enjoy the limelight or making life-changing decisions, so can often feel unheard. They can also put themselves last as they are too busy taking care of everyone else's needs. If you are in a relationship with a Queen of Cups, make sure they get some love and time to recharge before they burn out or breakdown.

At Work and Career

You will find the Queen of Cups in any arena of emotional and intuitive healing. This is an archetype who is great at working in a team on their own as long as they feel as though they are using their talents for the greater good. Any realm of personal development, spiritual counselling and support, healing, and working with children will be areas that the Queen of Cups will feel perfectly at home in.

Working in a team, the Queen of Cups will be the one looking out for everyone else's welfare and will often hold the emotional temperature of the team, so pay close attention to the Queen of Cups if you are a team leader or manager. They will tell you early on with their body language and words if things aren't as good as you think they are. They understand the importance of safe space and will only work in positions and for companies that foster this for their employees.

The Mystic at work can often be overlooked because they are the ones doing the work, not seeking the approval. They are often highly emotionally invested in their workplace and the people in it and big changes in the workplace can rattle them a lot. They do not like drama at work, and if there is any instance of bullying or issues with co-workers that can lead them to want to quit and find something new rather than stay and try to work things out.

Indicators that you are a Queen of Cups/Mystic archetype

- You make your decisions via your intuition
- Naturally empathic and have developed your skills throughout your life

- Has the ability to help others navigate their own psychic gifts
- Highly tuned in to the needs of others
- Very drawn to spiritual teachings and mystery traditions
- Speaks from the heart and third eye chakras
- Understands people on an energetic level
- Understands when to use their gifts and when not to get involved

Queen of Cups Strengths

- Wise
- Can communicate without needing words
- Connects well with others
- Natural humanitarian
- Responsible with their gifts
- Compassionate
- Lives to be of service to spirit
- Heals relationships and hearts

Queen of Cups Shadow Side

- Flaky
- Fearful of maltreatment from others
- Elitist
- Ungrounded
- Emotionally guarded
- Disconnected from reality
- Emotionally manipulative
- Martyr

The Queen of Cups Archetype in a Tarot Reading

Identifying the tarot court as either an aspect of yourself playing out or another person is something that can trip up even the most experienced tarot

reader. When the Queen of Cups comes up in a tarot reading, be on the lookout for these behaviours as identifiers:

- A highly intuitive individual who always seems to know what is going to happen before it does or who has other intuitive/psychic gifts that they are owning and using.

- Motivation—A person acting from a space of self-care and nurturing through acts of self-love.

- Someone who is emotionally manipulating people to get what they want, especially through guilt or emotional abuse.

If the Queen of Cups comes up in a position that requires an outcome, action, or the next step forward, consider these actions as suggestions to move into the archetype's power:

- Ask yourself—Am I listening to my intuition in this situation or am I just going to ignore it and do what I want anyway? (Note that you will likely repeat the same cycle until you learn to listen to your intuition.)

- Learn to embrace your emotions as gifts and learn how to protect and control them through intuitive and psychic development.

- Dive deeper than what has been offered on the surface. There is more to be considered here before you move forward.

- Ask—What would the Oracle of Delphi do? Work with the mythology of the archetype to gain in-depth answers and options for moving forward.

THE KNIGHT OF CUPS

Keywords

- Romantic
- Intoxicating
- Passionate
- Focused

- Artistic

- Expressive

- Daring

- Charming

Everyday Witch Tarot and Bad Bitches Tarot

Astrology—Pisces

The Knight of Cups holds dominion over the twelfth house of astrology, which is the house of mysticism and hidden secrets. This astrological house is connected to all of the magic and divine secrets of the universe. Knight of Cups people are often called to work with a higher power. This is sort of the perfect card for all diviners, as they are really attracted to the secrets of life. It is also the house of self-reflection and self-sabotage, which are the two sides to the same coin.

Archetype—The Romantic—The Lover and Casanova

The Knight of Cups as the Romantic is a sensitive idealist. Though they are literally the sexiest thing walking, they can also be rather forgetful and elusive. They are hopeless romantics that believe that love conquers all. Their personal holy grail is the perfect love. The Romantic is the type of person who gets completely swept up in love—reality be damned. Who cares about the real world when they are having such an exquisite time romancing a new partner? They are the types who will do anything for the person they are with and take great pride in being able to live up to their well-earned reputation. They often hold love and their lovers up on a pedestal and look at past relationships through rose-coloured glasses.

The Romantic archetype are also dreamers and artists, which is a perfect expression for all of the love that they feel. They find beauty all around them. People are really drawn to this person because they will look at you with such passion in their eyes, you will want to come along and dream with them. They tend to do everything in life with creative and expressive flare.

If their creative energy and need for connection is not channelled into something positive, they can become addicted to whatever they feel is going to fill the hole. They are always chasing something that is out of their grasp, but in truth, they are in love with the yearning, the chase, and the freshness of the unexplored.

In Love and Relationships

The Knight of Cups/Romantic is always seeking the perfect relationship, the one, their other half, their soul mate, twin flame, and someone who is of course of equal hotness to themselves. Finding that person is their quest and purpose in life. Heavens knows what they are going to do when they actually find that person though, because sticking around is not really their MO. When they think they have found the one, they suddenly realise that it was in fact an illusion and off they go seeking again.

They are also the emotional rescuer, someone who wants to feel needed. They want to be the hero and will find people that will validate their romantic gestures and efforts. They tend to be introspective and feel deeply, and can be wounded by the people they are in love with very easily.

All knights are linked to the element of fire. When the Knight of Cups taps into their fire, they can be harsh with their words and know just what to use to cripple the other person emotionally. Along with this fire comes the drama that is often attached to the Knight of Cups in their relationships. They want to feel all of the things with every fibre of their being, even if it is not bringing out the best in themselves or their partner.

The Romantic will often go back to ex-loves and have rose-coloured glasses when it comes to their past lovers. They even hold the person that they are with up against their elevated images, which has no base in reality but gives them an excuse to disregard someone and move on with little guilt.

At Work and Career
Knight of Cups people tend to have more than one creative passion and have an impressive toolkit of skills. They know how to use many aspects of creativity, from design suits to computer programs, visual storytelling, and the use of words. These knights often succeed when they are part of a creative team or when they work for themselves. If they are creative entrepreneurs, they will need someone to help them stay motivated or will have to outsource the work they don't want to do, such as accounting and sales. They want to do what they love and what they are good at and that is about it.

The Romantic can be really fickle and hard to get to commit to a project or job long term. They are not ones to do anything that needs a lot of analysing and attention to detail, so if you are working with a Knight of Cups, balance out your team with some practical personnel to help get things done. The Knight of Cups does not like rules and red tape and can be frustrated when things are not flowing. They are also not the easiest to manage and coach if they are having a bad day.

They can tend to stir up drama at work and will enjoy gossiping and can even be the type to start the drama. If they have a falling out with a leader or management at work, there is no way they will return to that work place. They won't resolve things with the people they feel have wronged them.

There is NO place that the Romantic feels is off limits when it comes to pursuing a lover, so this archetype has no problem getting busy with co-workers, bosses, and employees. Even better if it is breaking some company rules—it makes it all the hotter.

Indicators that you are a Knight of Cups/Romantic archetype

- You are a huge romantic and love to be in love
- No one is right for you, finding fault in your relationships
- The chase is sweeter than the capture
- You move around a lot in love, work, and life and it is always linked to how you are feeling
- Loyal to the love of your life, even if that is yourself or a project you are working on
- Experiences intense desires and dreams, but can find it hard to manifest them into reality
- Feels misunderstood by authority figures.

Knight of Cups Strengths

- Romantic
- Expressive with their love
- They push people outside of their comfort zone
- Uninterested in the status quo
- Trail blazers in the arts
- They don't settle

Knight of Cups Shadow Side

- Loves to play the game and treats love like a competitive sport
- Detached from the heart of love
- Gets involved in dramatic situations in all areas of life
- Swings from fantastic to doomed with little middle ground
- Matures later due to lack of stability

The Knight of Cups Archetype in a Tarot Reading

Identifying the tarot court as either an aspect of yourself playing out or another person is something that can trip up even the most experienced tarot

reader. When the Knight of Cups comes up in a tarot reading, be on the lookout for these behaviours as identifiers:

- A smooth talking, romantic person that stares into your soul.

- A person who has a reputation for leaving a trail of broken hearts.

- A temperamental being who does not like their fantasy spoiled or for people to rain on their parade.

- A person who is constantly chasing a fantasy in love and not something sustainable. This person often sees all aspects of life through rose-coloured glasses, not just relationships.

If the Knight of Cups comes up in a position that requires an outcome, action, or the next step forward, consider these actions as suggestions to move into the archetype's power:

- Ask yourself—Am I looking for something real or a fantasy that I am holding onto? Am I running away from emotional commitment?

- Learn to express your heart, your desires, your needs. This can be done through the written word, art, music, dance. Find your romantic voice and allow it some air time.

- Follow your heart and finally take action when it comes to the things you love.

- Ask—What would Casanova/Romeo/Juliet do? Work with the characters of the archetype or pop culture representations to gain in-depth answers and options for moving forward.

THE PAGE OF CUPS

Keywords

- Family orientated
- Emotionally open
- Imaginative
- Connected
- Transformative

- Charismatic

- Sensitive

Triple Goddess Tarot and Mucha Tarot

Astrology:

No fixed astrological assignment. The Empath/Page of Cups can be any aligned to any of the water zodiac signs: Cancer, Scorpio, or Pisces. They embody all of them.

Archetype—The Empath

The Page of Cups is extremely sensitive, which can be a gift if they are in an environment where it is embraced and supported. They wear their heart and the entirety of their emotional gamut on their sleeves. They are easily hurt and take words to heart. It can take a long time for them to heal from an emotional wound. Most importantly, people who have friends, children, lovers and family members who are the Empath will do well to encourage them to develop their skills and learn to manage their amazing energy so that they are not overwhelmed by the world but feel more self-empowered.

The Empath wants to learn everything that is connected to energy, love, emotion, and beauty as this is the language that they natively understand. They are a student of the arts, poetry, and painting. They love bodies of water and are children of the ocean. The Page of Cups will need a body of water to recharge and cleanse their energy regularly above regular hygienic bathing.

This archetype can easily get depressed or have nightmares if they are taking on too much energy that does not belong to them or if they do not know how to control their natural empathic gifts. Empaths need to have some grounding practices to help balance out their levels so that they don't take on everything around them and take everything personally.

The Empath is the kind of person that finds being around people, crowds, strange places, and loud noises the hardest. This is because Empaths are energetic and emotional sponges. They can't help but take in what is going on around them. It is as natural as breathing. To remedy this, Empaths benefit from good energetic hygiene and a lot of recharge time.

While Empaths can carry their gifts to adulthood, many find that they were forced to shut their gifts down for survival. It is easier to identify an Empath as a child than in an adult. Throughout their lives, Empaths will learn the skills of the other court cards through the knights (action), queens (nurturing), and kings (leading). They are like the raw element of their suit and therefore carry the most elemental power, which in the page's case is water/emotional.

In Love and Relationships

The Page of Cups can find codependent relationships very attractive because they need the security of another person to keep them safe. They are total balls of love though and give 100 percent of themselves to their relationships. They are such sweet beings when they give love and will naturally know what their partner needs without being told at any given moment.

They can be emotionally reliant on others as well and will seek out approval and constant reassurance that they are loved. They are a relationship chameleon and will go with the flow and be easily lead, by the other person. Being an emotional powerhouse, they can often be a little needy and will have a million triggers, so nearly anything can tip them off, especially if they are feeling overwhelmed.

If they have done little work on their gifts, they are going to be a handful for most people as they can be intense. Because of all of the energy they absorb, they can find it hard to communicate what their needs are, as they are not entirely sure if what they are feeling actually belongs to them or not at times. One of their secret weapons to get their way is to throw an Oscar award–winning tantrum.

Parents, family members, and partners of an Empath will do extremely well to get to understand their Empath's gift. Each Empath will experience their gift in a different way, so talking to them as though it is the most natural thing in the world and that you are on their side will yield positive results for everyone involved. Once there is understanding and open communication, parents can assist with the protection and development of their Empath and partners and family members can encourage that they lean into their strengths and develop their talents.

At Work and Career

The Empath needs to feel good about the work that they are doing and will need to be praised for their work often. They also need to feel safe. They tend to drift off and start a lot of creative projects but not finish them. They are natural artists and the type of people who had their first set of drums or guitar at a very young age and can play multiple instruments. If this is nurtured in them, they carry this gift throughout their lives, but they can also pick up their craft after years of not using it and it was like they never stopped.

This archetype will find the hustle and bustle of working in a big city or for a large corporation overwhelming if they are not able to control their abilities. It will simply be too much for them. They would rather have a small business working from home or be surrounded by people who are creative and who understand them than have a steady paycheck.

Indicators that you are a Page of Cups/Empath archetype

- Strong empathic gifts since childhood
- Have had or are in a codependent relationship (note that this relationship can be any relationship: a sibling, parent, or friend, not just a lover)

- Believe that love is all or nothing
- Constantly working on boundaries around energy and emotions
- Find it hard to take responsibility for failures in life

Page of Cups Strengths

- Can get a read on things that no one else can
- Extremely imaginative and has unlimited resources for creativity
- Loves with their whole being
- Cares deeply about the well-being of their community, family, and nature
- Will take care of you without you even needing to ask
- Upfront with how they are feeling

Page of Cups Shadow Side

- Will sulk when they don't get what they want
- Unsure of their identity outside of a relationship
- Unsure of how to cope with the world
- Wants to escape often
- Blames others for faults

The Page of Cups Archetype in a Tarot Reading

Identifying the tarot court as either an aspect of yourself playing out or another person is something that can trip up even the most experienced tarot reader. When the Page of Cups comes up in a tarot reading, be on the lookout for these behaviours as identifiers:

- A person who expresses their emotions openly without any filter, which can be a good thing, but some may find it confronting.
- A person who is very intuitive and feels energy from people and places naturally. This can also come up as someone who is highly empathic but finds it hard to put all of the emotions into words. Sometimes it comes up as anxiety or sadness. If those people can learn to connect their empathic energies to their throat chakra with safe people, there

can also be an opportunity to heal, as many of these people were told as children that what they are feeling is wrong.

- An emotionally immature person or someone who lacks a lot of self-understanding.

If the Page of Cups/Empath comes up in a position that requires an outcome, action, or the next step forward, consider these actions as suggestions to move into the archetype's power:

- Ask yourself—Am I the emotional barometer of the room that I am in? For example, if I am in a bad mood, does everyone else feel it, suffer and then come down to my level too?

- Learn to care about the feelings of other people. For those people where this does not come naturally, it will open many doors of understanding for you.

- Meet the obstacle or action with love and compassion first, foremost, and with as much enthusiasm as you possibly can. There is never too much love out there in the world.

- Ask—What would my heart do? Work with the embodiment of our emotions in this physical world. Sit with your heart and connect with your inner Empath.

THE KING OF WANDS

Keywords
- Hotheaded
- Daring
- Driven
- Visionary
- Challenging
- Committed
- Tenacious
- Disruptive

Triple Goddess Tarot and Everyday Witch Tarot

Astrology—Leo

The King of Wands is the ruler of the fifth house of astrology, which is the house of recreation, fun, romance, procreation, creativity, and children.

Archetype—The Entrepreneur

The Entrepreneur is going to create the life that they want and will have little time for anyone who is not on the same page or cannot get behind their vision. If you openly doubt them, they don't really care, they will just focus and succeed anyway. They have dared to try more times than most and even though there may be failed businesses in their past, they cannot conform to a job just because they need one. Life is not about having the same job or routine until the day they die; life is about doing things their way.

People love being around this archetype as they hold an infectious aura and a lifestyle many idolise. They have big energy which people can sense a mile off and they raise other peoples' vibrations just be being close to them. The King of Wands is engaging and inspiring. People feel better, warmer, and ready to take on the world when they are around them because they simply shine, all the time.

The King of Wands has an intuitive pulse on what people and the market need and are usually seen as untraditional by those who are happy doing things the way they have always been done. Want to insult this archetype? Call them ordinary. (Go on, I dare you.) They will happily be responsible for their failures in a business as long as they can reap the rewards of their successes too. Most risks are well and truly worth it and they love walking the fine line between brilliance and madness.

In Love and Relationships

The King of Wands/Entrepreneur needs to be with someone who is playful and that they see as just as attractive as they perceive themselves to be. They are going to be concerned with the way their physical body looks to the outside world, so you better be too if you are in a relationship with a King of Wands. They want to be "that" couple that people look at with jealousy in their eyes, even if things are not so crash hot behind closed doors.

The King of Wands is a constant flirt. It is their natural way of being and communicating with people. They demand attention. Whether good or bad, they don't really care so long as they are getting it. They are very aware of any reflective surface around them to check themselves out, and they know which angles of their faces are their best. The King of Wands can tend to have out of control egos if they are not balanced in any way. They live to be around people and will always be the one commanding and leading the conversation.

This tarot archetype wants a relationship that is going to support their success and may often leave their partners and family when the phone rings with a business call or miss out on birthdays and holidays. They often justify this with the notion that they are providing for their family and creating a lifestyle that they all deserve, even if their partner has a different idea of what is a desirable lifestyle. If you are in a relationship with this archetype, knowing what you are agreeing to is vital. You may get to go to wonderful locations all over the world in finery, but you may also not be the most important thing to your partner and may be left to do many things on your own.

The King of Wands is naturally drawn to children and will want children of their own (if for no other reason than to pass on their incredibly good looks … I kid, mostly). The hard part for the King of Wands in this is that they also want their independence. Balancing that scale is a constant battle for them. They are very family oriented but must have a good, healthy outlet for their need for recreation and creativity to make it work. Controlling or tying down this archetype in something too routine and mundane is just going to make them bolt.

At Work and Career

The Entrepreneur doesn't want to be the boss—they *need* to be the boss. If they are not in a leadership role, they soon will be. If they do not like the rules or think that they know better, there is going to be clashing of heads and fireworks going off in the office. They need to have creative freedom and want to make big changes. They are all about the big picture. If they are in a leadership role, get behind them or get out of their way.

The King of Wands as a child would have sold the most fundraising cookies every year or set up a car washing business on the weekends. More often than not this archetype will have had more than one business while growing up and loved nothing more than being the boss.

This archetype knows how to make the best out of any market situation and will quickly move to the next hottest trend and always seems to know where the next cash cow is going to be. They are also built for work starting many new companies and then selling them off for large sums of money, just to repeat the same thing in a different niche.

Indicators that you are a King of Wands/The Entrepreneur archetype

- You challenge ineffective authority figures without a second guess
- Had businesses and lemonade stands as a child

- Works to their full potential when in charge
- Not overly concerned with how others view you
- Takes risks for potentially large gains
- Ahead of trends and commercial markets
- Worked or works in start up businesses or owns own business

King of Wands Strengths

- Does what needs to be done
- Has great work ethic
- Thinks of the bigger picture
- Embraces change
- Inspirational
- Is a people person and often a philanthropist

King of Wands Shadow Side

- Ego may get out of control
- Can stretch themselves and relationships thin
- Changes too often and for no real good reason
- Ruthless in the name of business
- Uses people or sees them only for their usefulness
- Money and material things take priority

The King of Wands Archetype in a Tarot Reading

Identifying the tarot court as either an aspect of yourself playing out or another person is something that can trip up even the most experienced tarot reader. When the King of Wands comes up in a tarot reading, be on the lookout for these behaviours as identifiers:

- A person who is a naturally inspiring energy to be around. Someone who helps others ignite their own fires and gets them engaged in their own lives and world views.

- A person being an entrepreneur in an area of your life and not being afraid to go it alone. This can be anyone who is being a trailblazer in their own way.
- Observing actions that reflect caring for communities and the world, and working on humanitarian projects.

If the King of Wands comes up in a position that requires an outcome, action, or the next step forward, consider these actions as suggestions to move into the archetype's power:

- Ask yourself—Can I think and act bigger and do better? This is related to this king's ability to bring people together to make big changes.
- Be a leader that people want to follow, whether that is by cooling down the situation and bringing a level head or not being afraid to share your knowledge with others to empower them. This king is a natural at uniting people under a belief system (religious or not).
- Stand up for what you believe in and do not be afraid to be who you are.
- Ask—What would King Arthur do? Work with the character of the archetype and pop culture representations of that character to gain in-depth answers and options for moving forward.

THE QUEEN OF WANDS

Keywords
- Magnetic
- Powerful
- Influential
- Graceful
- Sensual
- Protective

- Fiery
- Entitled

Bad Bitches Tarot and Steampunk Tarot

Astrology—Aries

The Queen of Wands is the lady of the first house of astrology, which is the house of self-identity, the physical body, self-expression, personality, and self-discovery.

Archetype—The Performer

The Performer will feel like they are on stage at all times and they are the star. They are the actors, actresses, musicians, and artists. They are the life of the party and are naturally charismatic. Heads turn when the Queen of Wands walk into ANY room. They are likely to be the most popular person anywhere they go and will often be seen in the socialite papers drinking and dining with everyone who has connections. They know who they are and are very comfortable with themselves. There is an air of star quality about them. The Performer is concerned with social status, appearances, and social etiquette. They have a reputation to uphold and will make decisions across their entire life to keep up with their brand, even if it is not good for their health or happiness long term.

Being a natural chameleon, it can be difficult at first to know who this person really is as they are adept at putting on a show and hiding behind a mask. This can be used as a form of protection or as manipulation. The Performer is more likely than other court card archetypes to need validation from their peers and the public. They crave adoration from people they don't know and their loved ones alike.

The Queen of Wands/Performer is a creative and expressive person who experiences their journey to self-awareness and wholeness through embodying other people and playing out a variety of situations. If you are looking to get this archetype on the same page as you, know that they need to feel personally involved to be impacted or moved enough to take action on behalf of someone else.

The Queen of Wands is a competitive soul who is willing to take on any challenge that is presented to them. When there is difficulty in life, they are the one who rolls up their sleeves and says, "Bring it." If you ever try to tell this queen that they can't do something, they will give you the middle finger and say watch me! Part of this is bravado and the other part is that they have had to work hard for their position in life so are not afraid to go after something they deem worthy of their energy.

In Love and Relationships

The Queen of Wands can seem unattainable and will most likely have a large line of suitors just waiting in the wings to try to win their heart. They are a seductive soul who knows that they are a desired lover. People want to be them or be with them. They ooze sensuality, which is incredibly self-empowering and can often use their powers of seduction to get what they want. This can lead to the Queen of Wands attracting all of the wrong people in relationships, as they are attracted to their public face and not the real person underneath.

The Performer can hold a grudge for a very long time and will remember everything that was ever said or done in a relationship. Winning arguments with them can be too exhausting to even try. They do like their own time away from the relationship and will need their other half to give them some room to be an individual and be seen outside of their partnership. If you are in a relationship with a Queen of Wands and they want a weekend away with their best friends, it is advised you say yes. If denied they will find that release somewhere less constructive. You should feel privileged that they even considered asking you in the first place.

Authenticity is a challenge in relationships for this court card, this archetype as they can be more concerned about what their relationship looks like from the outside than what is going on underneath. They keep up appearances. For long-term relationships to be healthy and sustainable, this queen will have to be willing to do some committed personal work. Trying to change the Performer in a relationship is not going to work. They will have their priorities, which are usually their name in lights and award ceremonies, and will show what they are through their actions. If you are unable to accept that this is who and how they are, don't court them.

At Work and Career

The Queen of Wands is drawn to working with people who are going to give them the status and attention that they need. They want influence, accolades, and money. Depending on their set of values, they will use their ability to build considerable influence for the greater good or for purely selfish reasons. They are very savvy business people who leads their teams or business to success through unity and passion.

In a team of people, the Queen of Wands is more worried about cultural fit and the social life of everyone in the workplace than the actual work. They just want to like the people that they are working with and know that the company has a good social calendar and perks for their employees. This court card archetype usually leads team building activities and fundraisers in the workplace.

Because they are the Performer, they will need to be seen and heard, so any work where they get to stand in front of crowds of people and demand their undivided attention is going to be very appealing for them. That is if they are not working in the arts or building their own personal empire.

Indicators that you are a Queen of Wands/Performer archetype

- Been popular without effort for as long as you can remember
- You need the microphone wrestled from you at karaoke night
- Comfortable speaking to people from all walks of life
- You love attention and need to be working with people
- Concerned with the way the world views or judges you
- Your life tends to be extremely busy, dramatic, and full of people

Queen of Wands Strengths

- Radiates warmth
- Can instigate change with their huge influence
- Brings people together
- Inspiring for others to be around
- Connects and communicates with people well
- Wonderful storyteller

Queen of Wands Shadow Side

- Completely self-involved
- Obsessive
- Highly dramatic
- Can suffer from anxiety and other types of body stress
- Guarded

The Queen of Wands Archetype in a Tarot Reading

Identifying the tarot court as either an aspect of yourself playing out or another person is something that can trip up even the most experienced tarot reader. When the Queen of Wands comes up in a tarot reading, be on the lookout for these behaviours as identifiers:

- A person who uses their influence to do something about the causes they believe in.

- Motivation—Acting from a place of authenticity and allowing their light to shine.

- Someone who is not afraid of attention. This can be both healthy and unhealthy. A person who is not afraid of attention but is holding it in a positive way does not put down others or seek to steal someone else's glow. If someone is acting out to gain attention, there may be a need that is not being met.

- Someone who is hiding in a relationship or who is compartmentalising aspects of themselves and their lives. This person would rather escape into someone else's world than deal with their own reality.

If the Queen of Wands comes up in a position that requires an outcome, action, or the next step forward, consider these actions as suggestions to move into the archetype's power:

- Ask yourself—Can I find a better way of expressing who I am and what I need? Be flexible and able to adapt to many ways of doing things. Being rigid is not the way forward here.

- Sometimes you just have to put on a mask and smile through it, whether this is to stand up for yourself when asking for a promotion, or in front of a law or policy maker. It may be scary or uncomfortable but channel your inner performer, don't let them see you sweat.

- Give yourself a stage name and allow yourself to freely express what you need. Even Beyoncé and Lady Gaga have alter egos. There is a reason that masked parties and Halloween are times we give ourselves permission to let our inhibitions out.

- Ask—What would Margo Channing or Ally (*A Star is Born*) do? Work with the character of the archetype and pop culture representations of that character to gain in-depth answers and options for moving forward.

THE KNIGHT OF WANDS

Keywords

- Change
- Adventure
- Travel
- Spiritual pilgrimage
- Courage
- Faith
- Religious and or spiritual activities
- Initiative

Tarot Mucha and Everyday Witch Tarot

Astrology—Sagittarius

The Knight of Wands is the cavalier of the ninth house of astrology, which is the house of travel, ethics, law, philosophy, morality, and higher education.

Archetype—The Adventurer

The Adventurer is always on the move and planning their next exotic location to work and play in. They are not the kind of people to sit at a resort and lounge about—oh no, that is way too boring and a lost opportunity to discover some hidden gem of a restaurant that only the locals know about. Their mission is to experience life to the fullest, to surround themselves with as many different people and places they can in the most authentic way they can. They love to be active and feel like they are on their lifelong quest of knowing who they really are, which in my experience with the Knight of Wands people, has been by having a lot of sex, travelling, and running at the first sign of commitment.

These people cannot sit still and will often live in many places throughout their lives. The Knight of Wands wants to move out of home as soon as they can and will most likely move to another country, never to return to their hometown permanently again. The Adventurer doesn't own a lot of physical things while they are travelling extensively; memories mean more anyway. If they can't carry it, they won't buy it. But you can be sure their Instagram feed is a jealousy-inducing sight to behold.

The Adventurer will often be drawn to be part of many spiritual or religious paths. They are seeking the ultimate connection and this is one of the ways they can go about experiencing this. Joining churches, covens, groups, and spiritual communities feeds their need for something new or someone new all the time.

The Knight of Wands thinks that they are invincible. They are carefree and flexible and change doesn't phase them in the least. All of these things, along with their tales of exotic travel and crazy adventures, makes them very alluring. People are naturally drawn them. They are up for anything, once or twice, and are very adaptable, ever the social chameleon. They seem to have a million friends, but few very close friends. All of the moving about doesn't help with building lasting relationships.

In Love and Relationships

The Knight of Wands burns very brightly but not for very long. They are fireworks and summer love or that romantic hookup you had on vacation. They will seek people who want adventure and who want to come along for the ride. However they are the ones who are in charge of the party train, so their partner has to be okay with going with the flow and having things change at the drop of a hat.

Being the Adventurer, they view relationships and romantic love as just that, another adventure. They will look at how they can conquer their latest lover's desires and find their secrets just as though they were looking at climbing a mountain. Once they have climbed that mountain, however, they aren't likely to want to stay for long as they know there is another conquest to win just over the horizon.

The Knight of Wands is a yes person and will usually overcommit their energy, which, at times, can leave very little for their partner. They can be laying right next to you but a million miles away. If they have not done any real self-development, they are in for rocky relationships. They usually leave a trail of broken hearts and unrequited love behind them while they charge ahead, unaware of the devastation they leave in their wake.

At Work and Career

The Knight of Wands will not be the type of person who will go to college for years and then sit behind a desk for the rest of their life. They would rather be sleeping on their friend's couch and work for themselves than do that. The Knight of Wands will want a job where they have freedom and flexibility. If they feel as though they are getting told what to do too much, they are out. They hate playing by other peoples' rules and are not into doing the same thing every day, which is why any position that requires travel and constant change is perfect for them.

Working in a team with this archetype can be tricky. When they are on a roll, they are incredibly effective at getting things done, and their ability to adapt and change quickly make them assets in many professions, but they constantly need a challenge. They won't settle for good enough. Once they have mastered one role, they will be looking at something new or they will be on vacation all of the time.

Any role that has an element of competition will be highly attractive to the Adventurer as they love nothing but to throw themselves into competition. If they can make unlimited amounts of money, they are more than likely going to stick around too, because their goals will always be moving.

Indicators that you are a Knight of Wands/Adventurer archetype

- Interested in religion, philosophy, and spiritual paths from a young age
- Change rarely has a negative effect on you
- Problem-solving is a highly developed skill
- You have a lot of stamps in your passport
- You left home early and moved from your hometown
- Telling stories about your amazing adventures is second nature
- Relationships are thought of fondly, but you aren't ready yet to lay down roots

Knight of Wands Strengths

- Incredibly adaptable
- Highly motivational
- Is a bridge between people
- Open minded and inclusive
- Physically capable

Knight of Wands Shadow Side

- Doesn't clean up their emotional mess well
- Selfish
- Careless
- Immature
- Restless and unfulfilled

The Knight of Wands Archetype in a Tarot Reading

Identifying the tarot court as either an aspect of yourself playing out or another person is something that can trip up even the most experienced tarot reader. When the Knight of Wands comes up in a tarot reading, be on the lookout for these behaviours as identifiers:

- A person who is travelling a lot for work, travel and work abroad, or are constantly on the road.

- Observing someone who has experienced and been part of different spiritual paths and religions throughout their lives. Someone who is always seeking something bigger, something inside themselves and/or to understand the intelligent universe.

- A natural storyteller who is able to connect with people in an intimate way to better understand themselves. They are often the catalyst for people starting their own spiritual journeys as well.

If the Knight of Wands comes up in a position that requires an outcome, action, or the next step forward, consider these actions as suggestions to move into the archetype's power:

- Ask yourself—Am I really passionate about what I am doing with my life? This is a good way to check in to see if you are allowing yourself the time and energy to do what makes your heart and soul happy outside your worldly responsibilities.

- Take action now! Do the thing. Be in the moment and embrace it. This is especially true when the next step includes a plane ticket or moving geographical location.

- Ask—What would Indiana Jones do? Work with the character of the archetype and pop culture representations of that character to gain in-depth answers and options for moving forward.

THE PAGE OF WANDS

Keywords
- Fun
- Joyful
- Inquisitive
- Impulsive
- Irrational
- Cheeky
- Playful

Bad Bitches Tarot and Mucha Tarot

Astrology

No fixed astrological assignment. The Page of Wands can be any of the fire zodiac signs: Leo, Aries, or Sagittarius. They embody all of them.

Archetype—Peter Pan

Peter Pan is a hard one to pin down, literally. This ball of energy is always on the go and very rarely sits still. They have an off and on button—it is one or the other, all of the time. They are excitable people who have many, many things on the go all at once. They are drawn to creative and spiritual ventures and are extremely enthusiastic when it comes to spiritual progress and self-knowledge but don't really want to implement any of it because that means they will have to change and grow up.

They are always looking for something. Because they are at the beginning of their spiritual journey, being Peter Pan, this page often looks outside of themselves instead of inside. They are confident and self-assured, but they lack experience or knowledge to back their confidence up. Think of a dis-

ciple of any spiritual path at the beginning of their journey. They are into
everything and want to buy all of the tools, read all of the books, and start
all of the arguments and discussions but have little knowledge to really help
them get past one or two points.

The Page of Wands is full of joy and laughter. You can't keep this enthusiastic person down; they bounce right back up again and keep on going.
They can be theatrical, cruel, and superficial as well. Drama is their middle
name, so this can be either expressed in a healthy way or be rather toxic.
They crave attention like a flame needs oxygen and will get very destructive
if they aren't being seen and validated.

As soon as something becomes too serious or is no longer any fun, they
are out. If they are not having a good time, they don't see the point. People
tend to grow tired of this after a time, and the Peter Pan archetype may find
it hard to have deep connections because they are easily distracted and don't
like taking responsibility for their lives or actions. They always have a reason
why something is the way it is and an excuse or scapegoat or seven that they
are ready to rattle off in case they need to get out of something.

In Love and Relationships

Parents of a Peter Pan archetype will be constantly on the go or cleaning up
after their cheeky monkey. Getting this child to burn off their energy with
plenty of varied physical activity will aid them in finding some peace and
quiet later on. With healthy imaginations, these children will thrive in dance,
theatre, and sport. It is a good idea to watch your Peter Pan child as they can
easily become the ring leader child in their group with their incredible charm
and if they are not nurtured to understand other children, they may become
bullies or leaders of cliques.

The Page of Wands archetype as an adult is a very passionate lover and
partner. They are outspoken and like to argue. If there aren't fireworks,
shouting, and passionate make up sex, then there isn't love in their opinion.
They are likely to burn through a few relationships before they are ready to
leave the need for drama behind. They are quick to fall in love or lust with
someone and just as quick to fall out. They often have very healthy tempers.

At Work and Career

Peter Pan will find being an apprentice in anything that leads to knowledge or accolades very tempting but the actual work gruelling. The Page of Wands tends to have a lot of passion projects on the go, but the chances of them completing any of them are slim. The idea of the thing is always so much better than the reality. They are however, very good at getting others to do their work for them.

They are reactive and when something does not go their way at work, they are not going to be at all happy about it. Believe me, you will know just how unhappy they are. They don't keep their opinions to themselves. However, if they have managed to harness their power, they can be great problem-solvers. They can also suffer from foot in mouth disease and may not be able to stop themselves from saying something in anger that will get them in trouble.

Peter Pan is going to jump from job to job and be very likely to find get rich quick schemes very tempting. They will very easily ask for investment money from the people in their lives and will find someone to drain dry of resources for their next big idea.

Indicators that you are a Page of Wands/Peter Pan archetype

- Extroverted and comfortable with people from a young age
- People have always been drawn to you
- The class or workplace clown
- Many relationships with younger people, will often sire children with multiple mothers or fathers
- Money and stability are issues because you never stick to anything for very long
- Like to gossip and be in the thick of the drama
- Attention seeker

Page of Wands Strengths

- Optimistic in all areas of life
- Keeps up with technological and cultural changes
- Naturally aligned with cheering people up when they are down

- Sees the magic and joy in life
- Is always on an adventure or telling you about one

Page of Wands Shadow Side

- Unwilling to take responsibility for their life
- Slow to admit when they are wrong
- Rash when making decisions
- Can fire up people for the wrong reasons
- Runs away from anything challenging or hard

The Page of Wands Archetype in a Tarot Reading

Identifying the tarot court as either an aspect of yourself playing out or another person is something that can trip up even the most experienced tarot reader. When the Page of Wands comes up in a tarot reading, be on the lookout for these behaviours as identifiers:

- A person who just doesn't want to grow up.
- Temper tantrums, arguments, and people starting fights just for the heck of it.
- Observation of free expression. This comes in all forms but is done with a lot of gusto and energy no matter what the method.

If the Page of Wands comes up in a position that requires an outcome, action, or the next step forward, consider these actions as suggestions to move into the archetype's power:

- Ask yourself—Am I thinking outside the box? Am I making things more dramatic than they need to be? While this archetype has immature tendencies, they are also excellent at lateral thinking. Putting the energy needed to keep the drama at bay and putting it to more creative endeavours is highly suggested.
- See things from the space of the magic and joy of your inner child, when believing things was more important than knowing the truth, when you were able to use your imagination to transport yourself to anywhere and be anything.

- Ask—What would Peter Pan do? Work with the character of the archetype and pop culture representations of that character to gain in-depth answers and options for moving forward.

The King of Pentacles

Keywords

- Powerful
- Rich
- Practical
- Generous
- Materialistic
- Disciplined
- Reliable

Bad Bitches Tarot and Steampunk Tarot

Astrology—Taurus

The King of Pentacles is the patriarch of the second house of astrology, which is the house of values, ethics, self-worth, and personal belongings.

Archetype—The Manager

The Manager is a confident archetype that demands respect. This is usually because they hold power or money (or both) and this need for people to respect them can be misplaced or unjustified. They assume everyone values the same things that they do and do not even try to convince people of their perceived entitlement. They walk into the room like they own it, and with this archetype, they very well may own the entire building.

The King of Pentacles knows where to invest their time, money, and energy. They have an uncanny instinct with people and situations, and their advice is often sought as they are rarely wrong, especially if there is monetary gain or loss on the line. They know how to get just about anything to achieve their goals and are natural networkers because people want to know this person. They are born doers, but rather than being idealistic about their roles, they want to see results.

If there is an archetype in the tarot court that hates time wasters, it is the King of Pentacles. Time is money. When you come to them, you want to get straight to the point and hold the flattery, as it is not going to get you anywhere. The King of Pentacles also uses their words wisely. They know that listening and silence hold more power than most realise.

While the Manager can be as subtle as a sledgehammer, they have a warm side and are very protective of those who they choose to be in their tribe. The King of Pentacles has a dry sense of humour and will be laughing when no one else is. When they feel as though the people around them have shown their worth they will be very giving with their riches and want to help the people around them succeed.

In Love and Relationships

The King of Pentacles is the provider. If their loved ones need something, or even if they just want something, they will make it happen for them. They are not afraid to go after what they want. The Manager can tend to spoil the person that they are with. The way that this archetype shows love is usually through the material world. Gifts, trips, pampering, all of the things the human experience can want to experience will be given freely to the people they love.

The Manager can seem emotionless and insensitive, especially to outsiders, and will rarely share how they are feeling. They will find relationships that are sensible and feasible and like down-to-earth people. They are practical communicators who don't sugar coat things. This can come across as harsh or blunt, but they rarely mean it to. They are just to the point. It can take a lot to provoke this bull but when they get triggered you would do best to get out of the way, as they are a force to be reckoned with. They are more likely to avoid confrontation and change in a relationship if everything is working well enough and they are comfortable.

The King of Pentacles can also signify someone who has married for money, political reasons, or even an arranged marriage. There has to be a benefit somewhere to getting married, right?

At Work and Career

The King of Pentacles is the money person. They are the one with their name in the business and the Manager on their business card. They have access to the company's private jet, the designer wardrobe, and the "I could build a house with that" expensive watch. They differ from the Entrepreneur as the Manager is happy to work for someone else in a well established business. They will follow the rules, take the paths that have proven successful before, and plan their success with detail.

The King of Pentacles will consider the bottom line in all decisions around their career and business. They track and watch what is happening at work and are likely to surpass expectations when it comes to their key performance indicators and goals. They will want to have a clear career path and want to be promoted, praised, and rewarded in their work. They will often have an endgame in mind with their career, which usually sees them sitting in charge of large amounts of money, people, or both.

In business and in life this archetype will want to dominate. They play to win and are not the kind of person who can be swayed from their goals. This is also the card of real life kings and royalty.

Indicators that you are a King of Pentacles/Manager archetype

- Naturally able to save money
- Resourceful and know how to get what you need
- Like the finer things in life
- Good with large projects and a lot of moving parts
- Want quality over quantity
- Fantastic in management positions
- Holds self and others to high expectations
- Once you have decided, the course is set in stone

King of Pentacles Strengths

- Provides more than enough
- Shows love and appreciation
- Manages resources and money expertly
- Makes informed and smart decisions
- Good at the long game
- Listens well and consults others
- Organised

King of Pentacles Shadow Side

- Greedy
- Critical of others and self
- Impatient with people they deem unworthy
- Unable to change easily
- Withholding of emotions and love
- Feels there is never enough

The King of Pentacles Archetype in a Tarot Reading

Identifying the tarot court as either an aspect of yourself playing out or another person is something that can trip up even the most experienced tarot

reader. When the King of Pentacles comes up in a tarot reading, be on the lookout for these behaviours as identifiers:

- Someone who is being cautious and who wants to get a solid grasp on the situation before jumping in and making a decision.

- A money-honey or a person who is not afraid to be generous with their riches. The positive money-honey is a generous person who shares what they have and realises that people and relationships are worth more than cash. However, they can also risk financial ruin to keep up appearances or be someone who is using another just for their cash.

- Someone who is dedicated to working on their business or dreams. This person is highly dedicated, successful, and usually a bit of a workaholic.

If the King of Pentacles comes up in a position that requires an outcome, action, or the next step forward, consider these actions as suggestions to move into the archetype's power:

- Ask yourself—Am I taking responsibility for my life and situation? If there was ever a tarot archetype that was not afraid of responsibility, it is this one.

- Do the numbers, check your risks and blind spots, and only do what is practically sound. Simply doing something right is worth your investment.

- Ask—What would Gordon Gekko from *Wall Street* do? Work with the character of the archetype and pop culture representations of that character to gain in-depth answers and options for moving forward.

THE QUEEN OF PENTACLES

Keywords
- Nurturing
- Soft
- Compassionate
- Connected
- Open

- Abundant

- Loving

- Refined

Steampunk Tarot and Everyday Witch Tarot

Astrology—Capricorn

The Queen of Pentacles is the monarch of the tenth house of astrology, which is the house of social status and career.

Archetype—The Healer

The Healer is the most nurturing of the archetypes of the tarot court. They love nothing more than to care for people and help those who are in need. The Healer makes things better just by being themselves. They radiate an energy that puts other people at ease and at peace. They know all the right, sincere words to say and what needs to be done to fix everything from a broken heart to setting a broken bone.

This tarot archetype loves to provide comfort and warmth to people, which by extension often means that their homes are always open and they will feed their entire neighbourhood if needed. Their fridge is always full, the kettle is always ready to go on and the Healer loves it when they are sought out for comfort.

Their connection with the community that they are part of also means that this queen knows everyone's business and can often be very concerned with their social status. They know what is happening in all of their friends and families lives and will want to keep up with the comings and goings of their tribe. If they are not aligned or are in their shadow, they will happily use peoples' weaknesses against them, or when they are in need of help, exploit that opportunity. If they are working as a Healer for the social status, they can start to get big headed about their abilities.

In Love and Relationships

The Queen of Pentacles can be a little bit of a traditionalist. They like family, routine, and traditions that have been passed down from previous generations—especially the ones that they have fond memories of. They are natural caretakers and children will be drawn to them. Family is extremely important to this archetype and there is little they wouldn't do for people they consider their own.

People who have a Queen of Pentacles in their lives will know that they will open their heart and arms to just about anyone and this can be hard if you are chasing undivided attention from this tarot personality. As they are connected to many people, they will be well respected and often sought out by others with little time and energy for the people closest to them. The Queen of Pentacles needs to ensure that they care for their intimate and family relationships as well as taking care of those who need their gifts.

The Queen of Pentacles can be overprotective, smothering, and even downright jealous if they haven't done any real personal development work. They are sensual, sexy, and—being in tune with their own body—have a healthy sexual appetite. They know that there is much magic that can be done with sexual healing work.

At Work and Career

The Healer will use their resources, mind, and body to make the world a better place, whether directly as a doctor or nurse or by raising funds for a charity. They need to help others and it comes so naturally people are often blown away by the depth of their energetic reservoir. They simply will work until they cannot stand. The Healers hands are their greatest tool and they are not afraid to get them dirty. They don't want to lead from afar. They want to be right where the action is, making a real, lasting difference.

This queen works well with people and loves to connect with them, but when the pressure is on and it is time to work, social interactions become less important and they are all business. This is because many Healers are in a line of work where the choices they makes can have life altering repercussions. Nothing is more important than taking care of a person in need.

Indicators that you are a Queen of Pentacles/Healer archetype

- Always cared for people in their family and social circle
- Loves comfort and warmth
- Role played healing professionals and roles as a child such as doctor
- Wants to make people feel better
- Felt as if there was no other vocation or path in life but to be a healer
- Has had to do substantial healing in their lives or watched someone close be a survivor
- Wants to give to others what they didn't have themselves

Queen of Pentacles Strengths

- Never turns away someone in need
- Has a huge heart
- Has energetic endurance
- Adaptable to their environment
- Excellent in times of crisis
- Is often the heart of their community

- Knows what is really going on
- Humble

Queen of Pentacles Shadow Side

- Can develop a god complex
- Smothering
- Manipulating
- Arrogant about their abilities
- Unwilling to admit when they are at fault
- Often have a blind spot when it comes to their own need to heal
- Needs to be needed

The Queen of Pentacles Archetype in a Tarot Reading

Identifying the tarot court as either an aspect of yourself playing out or another person is something that can trip up even the most experienced tarot reader. When the Queen of Pentacles comes up in a tarot reading, be on the lookout for these behaviours as identifiers:

- A person who takes their friends and loved ones soup when they are sick or brews a calming tea for a friend.
- Someone connected to the elements of earth. They love to garden, will likely have their own vegetable and herb garden and knows their way around a kitchen. Not because they need to know how to cook and heal with food, they love doing it.
- Anyone who is in a mother role or is acting as such in your life or in the situation at hand.

If the Queen of Pentacles comes up in a position that requires an outcome, action, or the next step forward, consider these actions as suggestions to move into the archetype's power:

- Ask yourself—What needs healing/nurturing in this situation?
- Look to your community and network for the next step forward. Are you unwilling to ask for assistance? Receive as well as you are able to give.

• Ask—What would Florence Nightingale here do? Work with the character of the archetype and pop culture representations of that character to gain in-depth answers and options for moving forward.

THE KNIGHT OF PENTACLES

Keywords

- Loyal
- Enduring
- Responsible
- Dependable
- Protective
- Disciplined
- Trained

Bad Bitches Tarot and Triple Goddess Tarot

Astrology—Virgo

The Knight of Pentacles is the cavalier of the sixth house of astrology, which is the house of work, colleagues, health, and service to others.

Archetype—The Soldier

If you ever need someone to protect you, this is the tarot archetype you want to show up. The Soldier life is about service to a higher good and to their fellow people. There is nothing more worthwhile in their hearts and they will lay down their lives in that service. They are loyal and will be there long after everyone else has given up.

The Soldier will actively seek out groups of people with strong leaders to follow. If the cause is aligned to their natural desire to protect the people that they love it's even better. They believe in their duty to others through protective service and crave acceptance by their brotherhood.

The Knight of Pentacles is a long distance endurance Knight. They are in it for the long haul and lengthy hard work campaigns are where they shine. The Knight of Pentacles is cool, calm, and collected most of the time, but they still have the energy of the Knight (which is action)—they are just a little more hesitant to charge into battle than the other knights in the tarot court. This keeps the Soldier out of trouble more than the others and will also see them persisting long after everyone else has had to tap out.

The Knight of Pentacles is a patient, analytical being who loves nothing more than to stumble across something that needs fixing and be there until the issue is resolved. They love to get their hands dirty as they feel paralyzed and useless if they are not doing something to help.

In Love and Relationships

The Knight of Pentacles is not one to give up on a relationship when they have finally committed to one. When they give their heart to someone and can see a future with them they are rarely deterred from making that a reality. The Soldier may find that they are attracted to people that they can romantically rescue. They also have no hesitations in telling others about how they should fix their life and problems even if they have not asked for any help.

If you are making an effort and showing that you value their efforts, this tarot archetype will be in the relationship for the long haul. The Knight of Pentacles is conscious about their health and wants their partner to be as well.

The Knight of Pentacles can be a real perfectionist and this can manifest either inwardly or outwardly. They are usually very hard on themselves and feel like they can always do better or they project it onto their partner. If you are in a relationship with a Knight of Pentacles, you'd better hope that they didn't have dominating parents who were unusually hard on them, because that conditioning on top of their already well-developed natural critic can make for a very hard taskmaster in a relationship.

At Work and Career

This archetype is also a career person. The Knight of Pentacles wants to make a difference and to feel like they belong. They want to be depended on and have a dependable workplace in return. They are likely to feel very loyal towards their employers and team, even if they could be earning more money elsewhere. People matter more than money.

The Knight of Pentacles is going to take their time to complete their work but it is going to be perfection so it is worth the wait. They love to fix things, so remember that these people are great in problem-solving arenas and project planning. They love work with routine and structure. They are much more productive in a steady environment where they know what is expected of them and the people around them. Everything else could be going to hell in a handbasket, but as long as they know what they need to do and what they need to rally the team to get done, they will do it.

The Soldier is not afraid of tackling large projects and things that can seem insurmountable to most people. They know that all they need to do is to focus on the next step that they need to take, knowing that completing one step at a time leads to strong foundations and excellent work outcomes. This knight works exceptionally well in team environments where they are surrounded by people working towards the same goal. They can be idealistic about their work as it is a large part of their personal identity. This is seen in Knight of Pentacle people who work in any armed forces or that are activists for humanitarian causes.

Indicators that you are a Knight of Pentacles/Soldier archetype

- You will stand up to bullies without a second thought
- Believes people deserve protection and peace
- Once you are committed to something, you are all in
- Enjoys the feeling of belonging in a group or organisation
- Does well with routine and structure in life
- Wants to be part of something larger than themselves

Knight of Pentacles Strengths

- Does the work
- Strong-willed
- Takes pride in their role in society
- Will protect those they love
- Will be there after everyone else has left
- Doesn't give up
- Focuses on what they are doing

Knight of Pentacles Shadow Side

- Unable to see fault in people in power
- Rigid
- Perfectionist
- Has strong views bordering on extremism
- Will follow leaders without question
- Indoctrinated
- Unable to find their identity outside their work/archetype

The Knight of Pentacles Archetype in a Tarot Reading

Identifying the tarot court as either an aspect of yourself playing out or another person is something that can trip up even the most experienced tarot reader. When the Knight of Pentacles comes up in a tarot reading, be on the lookout for these behaviours as identifiers:

- The loyalist person you know, the friend who has always stuck by you, defended you and been there through everything. This person can also be a sibling, guardian, or lover. Loyalty will be one of their top defining character traits.
- Someone who has a planner (or ten) and sticks to their schedule. They have a day in the week for everything, plan their meals, workout regularly, and usually have a budget.
- A person who takes their time deliberately to make choices or to go outside what is required to be done. They will often go with the pack and make sure no one is left behind.

If the Knight of Pentacles comes up in a position that requires an outcome, action, or the next step forward, consider these actions as suggestions to move into the archetype's power:

- Ask yourself—Am I preparing to succeed or fail here? Look at your structure, routine and foundations of belief. Where are they leading you if you continue down the current path?
- What is the next step forward? Stop thinking about everything that needs to get done. Just focus on the very next thing on your list and do that. Once that is complete, focus on the next step and keep going.
- Ask—What would Captain John H. Miller do? (*Saving Private Ryan*) Work with the character of the archetype and pop culture representations of that character to gain in-depth answers and options for moving forward.

THE PAGE OF PENTACLES

Keywords
- Quiet
- Kind
- Meticulous
- Slow-moving

- Gentle
- Instinctive

Everyday Witch Tarot and Bad Bitches Tarot

Astrology—No fixed astrological assignment.

The Page of Pentacles can be any of the earth zodiac signs: Capricorn, Virgo, or Taurus. They embody all of them. The Page of Pentacles has unlimited potential like all children.

Archetype—The Naturalist

The Naturalist is a beautiful soul who would much rather be in the company of animals than people and adores being out in nature. They have likely brought home many stray or injured animals throughout their lives and pets have always been part of their lives. They often have an empathic connection with animals and will suffer as the animal suffers if one is injured or sick.

This tarot archetype understands so much that is being said without the need for words and, with their alignment to healing, knows when someone or something needs care. Naturalists are the people who mourn when a tree is cut down or an animal is injured or sick, even if it is in a movie.

The Page of Pentacles is quiet and predictable. They are slow moving in all aspects of their lives, always late and cannot be rushed out the door or indeed into or out of anything. They run on their own timetable and will take whatever time they need. They believe that anything worth doing takes time and rushing leads to mistakes. They will remind us, if we stop and allow them to, that life is meant to be experienced and that we should all take time to slow down.

Naturalists understand nature. They are perfectly okay with things that require a slow and steady approach. They are excellent with anything that involves a long term commitment.

The Page of Pentacles are very kinaesthetic. They love to get their hands dirty and learn by doing. They will often be up in a tree, getting muddy or playing with their favourite animal. They are into simplicity, simple minded but not stupid, and will offer simple solutions. They offer the next step in a process, not the big picture, because as they see it, the next step is all you need to know.

In Love and Relationships

This archetype wants safety and security. These people do not take risks. Why should they? They know what they have and what is going to happen, so why bother? They take a long time to make decisions and need their space to do so. Pushing or crowding them to make a choice will only set them back further.

They are going to have "fur babies" and they treat any of their animal kin as family. These relationships are just as serious as any other human chosen significant other, family member or friend—if they choose to have a significant other at all.

The Page of Pentacles is a natural worrier, which is why they don't take risks. You know what you get and what to expect with a Page of Pentacles. They are extremely loyal partners but can tend to be a bit lazy and let things get stagnant in a relationship. They can tend to turn into a bit of a couch potato and can slip into bad routines easily.

In Work and Career

The Page of Pentacles wants to be working with their hands and are not ones for being kept indoors all day. They are also not overly interested in a lot of social or personal contact at work, so you won't find them gossiping at lunch time.

The Naturalist will want to fix, heal, and nurture their work. They will need to be able to take their time and have a hands-on approach to getting the job done. While they may not complete the task as quickly as everyone else, they will do an amazing job and will be the one to bring a project back to life or an animal back from the brink of death. They will commit their time to what they believe in.

Indicators that you are a Page of Pentacles/Naturalist archetype

- You love being barefoot and probably hated wearing shoes as a child
- Naturally attuned to/empathic connection with animals since you were a child
- You have a small group of friends and prefer one on one time vs large crowds
- Comfortable with silence
- Like to work with your hands, especially with animals and nature
- Enjoy being outdoors
- Prefer pets/animals to most people

Page of Pentacles Strengths

- Extremely caring
- Grounded
- Open
- Gentle
- Wonderful with nonverbal communication
- Excellent with animals

Page of Pentacles Shadow Side

- May have difficulties with personal boundaries and standing up for themselves
- Disappears within themselves
- Can tend toward isolation from their community
- Finds it hard to communicate
- Human friendships can be hard to make and maintain
- Feels pain acutely for fauna and flora

The Page of Pentacles Archetype in a Tarot Reading

Identifying the tarot court as either an aspect of yourself playing out or another person is something that can trip up even the most experienced tarot reader. When the Page of Pentacles comes up in a tarot reading, be on the lookout for these behaviours as identifiers:

- When everyone else is sitting around debating and talking about solving a problem, this person is already doing something about it.
- When there are tense situations, this is someone who will actively seek out pets and animals as a way to help balance and calm their energy and the people around them.
- A person who likes comfortable, practical clothing and footwear or doesn't like to wear shoes at all.

If the Page of Pentacles comes up in a position that requires an outcome, action, or the next step forward, consider these actions as suggestions to move into the archetype's power:

- Ask yourself—Am I being honest with myself and others? This tarot archetype doesn't even think of lying, beyond being wrong. They don't like to complicate things with lies.
- Reflect on whether or not you are making things more complicated than they need to be. Look for the simple solution or next move. Often it is just what is needed.

- Ask—What would Queen Tara do? (*Epic*) Work with the character of the archetype and pop culture representations of that character to gain in-depth answers and options for moving forward.

THE KING OF SWORDS

Keywords

- Brilliant
- Intelligent
- Precise
- Focused
- Expert
- Macrocosmic
- Genius
- Logical

Steampunk Tarot and Everyday Witch Tarot

Astrology—Aquarius

The King of Swords is the King of the eleventh house of astrology, which is the house of causes, communities, friends, groups, and unorthodox thinking.

Archetype—The Scientist/The Specialist

The archetype of the Scientist is a forward thinking individual who wants to make the world a better place and has big ideas of how to make that happen. They are ahead of their time and it is these people that change the world, push humanity forward, and develop new technology. They know that knowledge is power. They are incredibly logical in their approach and find it hard to deal with irrational people. This is the person you go to when you need a very specialised type of information or help. They are likely to be at the top of their field and highly educated and/or gifted.

Others may dismiss this archetype as a nutty professor, especially those who are not anywhere near their wavelength or level of intelligence. The King of Swords is used to being misunderstood and the odd one out but they are so unconcerned about that aspect of life they rarely notice. They can be seen as a bit radical by others, especially those who do not like change.

The Scientist is the idealistic leader who has a motto, vision, and model that they live and rule by. They will hold ALL up to this standard, which can make them impossible to please. They have no problem with being assertive and speaking out, especially when there is what they deem to be injustice happening. They will defend their ideals without a second thought and believe in order and peace.

The Scientist isn't just a big picture person, they are the biggest picture person. They build and re-envision institutions and cultural ways of thinking. Think of someone like Galileo, Dr. Martin Luther King Jr., Bill Nye, Marie Curie, Emmeline Pankhurst, or Elon Musk.

In Love and Relationships

If you can pry the King of Swords away from whatever world problem they are solving, their mind is probably still ticking away. They can be rather aloof and their lack of presence can be irritating. If you are in a relationship with a King of Swords, you may not see them for days on end while they lock themselves away to do their life's great work or work on something new.

Partners of this archetype will need to be okay sharing the love that the Scientist has for their work and for the people in their lives. They believe that the greatest way they can show their love is by making the world better for those they care for, through service.

The King of Swords is very ambitious and needs to have a partner who is happy to follow them in their direction and vision in life. They find intelligence very attractive. They are fair partners, as long as you are being logical, and by logical I mean their logic. They can be very hard on their partner and have very high expectations of them. This is a reflection of the high expectations they have on themselves but it is not always easy to live with. They love a good debate and would rather spend the rest of their lives with their best friend than anyone else.

At Work and Career

The King of Swords is going to be attracted to anything that helps the world become a better place. They will also need to have influence in their positions at work and will climb up the leadership ladder quickly. They often have very specific specialisations within their chosen profession and have knowledge that sees them sought out for.

They are unwavering in their work and will often forget to eat, sleep, or bathe when they are on a roll. This king will happily devote their lives to their vision and work and if they are working in a grounded and aware consciousness, will share their knowledge and teach others with the idea that more brilliant minds can do more good. If they are not self-aware, they will tend to become hermitted away and everything else in their lives but work will fall apart.

If you want to change the world, this is the tarot archetype you want to hire, consult, work with, and learn from.

Indicators that you are a King of Swords/Scientist archetype

- You were excited to open science kits at birthdays
- School was something you looked forward to
- Have always been interested in intricate details of how the universe works

- Consider the big picture in all things
- When working on a project, everything else disappears
- Educated in your field and respected by peers
- Wants to change the world
- Been curious about the why and how since childhood

King of Swords Strengths

- Believes in their abilities, themselves and their work
- A visionary
- Open to change, challenges, and new ways of doing things
- Helps others open their minds
- Moves society and technology forward
- Able to make real changes in the world
- Inspires others to create change

King of Swords Shadow Side

- Ungrounded and aloof
- Avoids practical life things like laundry
- Can be unrealistic with people and their vision
- Cold
- Arrogant
- Too rational, may need practices to reconnect to their heart
- Cynical
- Extreme

The King of Swords Archetype in a Tarot Reading

Identifying the tarot court as either an aspect of yourself playing out or another person is something that can trip up even the most experienced tarot reader. When the King of Swords comes up in a tarot reading, be on the lookout for these behaviours as identifiers:

- A person who is actively sought out for expert advice, whether that is looking to gain guidance from an expert or being the expert in the situation.

- An extremely well intelligent individual who is not afraid to upset the status quo or throw a spanner in the works. They care about getting things right over being popular.

- A person who is very focused on one thing, maybe a little too much.

If the King of Swords comes up in a position that requires an outcome, action, or the next step forward, consider these actions as suggestions to move into the archetype's power:

- Ask yourself—What details have I possibly missed? Go over things with a clear mind and really check the little things.

- Leave your emotions and biases on the shelf and look at things logically.

- Ask—What would Spock do? (*Star Trek*) Work with the character of the archetype and pop culture representations of that character to gain in-depth answers and options for moving forward.

THE QUEEN OF SWORDS

Keywords

- Fair
- Impartial
- Honest
- Direct
- Clear
- Articulate
- Benevolent/malevolent

Bad Bitches Tarot and Tarot Mucha

Astrology—Libra

The Queen of Swords is the queen of the seventh house of astrology, which is the house of partners, marriage, relationships, and connections with the public.

Archetype—The Judge

Honest, fair, and sharp as a tack, the Judge archetype is emotional intelligence personified. The Judge partners the intelligence that is the sword element (air) with nurturing and leading through the heart (the station of the queen). They are very aware of their emotions, their thoughts, and their words. They know that the mind and heart when connected can be an unstoppable power for change. On the flip side, if the Judge has a blocked heart, this archetype can be cold and extremely cruel, verbally mowing down people and manipulating to their own selfish ends.

Socially, the Judge can be identified as the person who everyone in your social circle has on speed dial for emergencies, counsel, and solving problems.

They are natural born mediators who can help bring people together who have trouble communicating in a clear, direct way.

The Queen of Swords does not take any shit and can see through it from a mile away. One look into your eyes and you will feel stripped. While this gives this archetype the best tools to be able to rule fairly, it can also give them the reputation of being harsh, cruel, and uncaring—mostly from the people who are being called out.

They understand that words have power, that they can harm or heal. This is not the archetype that you go to if you want to be coddled. This is the person you go to for the truth and honesty.

They are adaptable and open, being able to see an issue or problem from many angles. They will try to find a solution that is going to benefit all parties. This archetype has the communication on lock down and they have an extremely quick wit and usually a broad vocabulary.

In Love and Relationships

The Queen of Swords has a talent for using their quick wit and mind to enable them to fire rapid, hard hitting shots in an argument, but it also can make them quite the life of the party if they have someone to banter with. The Queen of Swords wants a partner who is loyal, fair, and intelligent. Lying to anyone is never a good idea, but lying to this archetype if you are in a relationship with them—that is a really bad idea. You will get caught.

The Queen of Swords will shower their lover with compliments that are true poetry to appreciate when their partner goes above and beyond for them. They are extremely affectionate and gracious. If they come across as cold, it is just that you do not know them well. The Queen of Swords also likes the finer things in life, including their relationships. It has to be the best. Relationships are their sanctuary where they can be real and express who they really are without judgement.

While this archetype can seem like they have solid armour they take words spoken to them, and about them, to heart. This is one of the reasons they are so linguistic. It is also their weakness in interpersonal relationships, as their ability to be emotionally intelligent about situations that hit close to home becomes harder to navigate.

At Work and Career

The Queen of Swords will often gravitate towards work where they are in a leadership position, but also one that connects with other people, especially those that network with a lot of people or puts them in a place of public influence.

When working with this archetype it is highly recommended to communicate clearly and often and not to sugar coat things during rough patches. They can be excellent managers as they are able to motivate and mediate teams well while still being able to do the work required.

As people seek out the Queen of Swords for advice and most importantly their ruling in areas of their lives, there are professions that this archetype is going to gravitate towards.

Indicators that you are a Queen of Swords/Judge archetype

- You are on speed dial for your friends when they have an issue
- Natural born peacekeeper and referee
- Good at debating
- Enjoy the written and spoken word
- Well read in a number of subjects
- Critical thinking is easy and natural
- Quick witted and verbose

Queen of Swords Strengths

- Wants what is fair for all
- Fantastic communicator
- Lateral thinker
- Trustworthy
- Values people
- Understands people and their underlying motivations
- Keeps secrets well
- Fantastic negotiator

Queen of Swords Shadow Side

- Cruel and cutting
- Judgemental
- Can be heartless and cold
- Intimidating
- Manipulative
- Disconnected from feelings

The Queen of Swords Archetype in a Tarot Reading

Identifying the tarot court as either an aspect of yourself playing out or another person is something that can trip up even the most experienced tarot reader. When the Queen of Swords comes up in a tarot reading, be on the lookout for these behaviours as identifiers:

- A person who keeps their cards close to their chest or who is not going to add their opinions in gossip. While they remain silent, they are absolutely paying very close attention to what people are saying.
- The walking, talking BS detector in your life. This person is very hard to successfully lie to and has a way of seeing directly into your true soul.
- A quick witted, silver tongued person who can talk their way out of or into just about anything and has a come back for everything.

If the Queen of Swords comes up in a position that requires an outcome, action, or the next step forward, consider these actions as suggestions to move into the archetype's power:

- Ask yourself—What is the outcome that is the most balanced and fair for all? While it is true that you cannot please everyone all of the time, you can try to bring some balance in.
- Be open to not taking a side. Look at staying open to different perspectives and points of view.

• Ask—What would Judge Judy do? While you could argue she is a real person and not a character to explore, television is always just a little made-up and she is really a perfect, well known example of this archetype.

THE KNIGHT OF SWORDS

Keywords

- Defender
- Action oriented
- Sacrifice
- Powerful
- Primal
- Empowered
- Swiftness

Triple Goddess Tarot and Bad Bitches Tarot

Astrology—Gemini

The Knight of Swords is the knight of the third house of astrology, which is the house of communication, logic, communities, writing, teaching, and siblings.

Archetype—The Warrior

The Warrior is a true knight, ready to charge into any battle and start swinging their giant sword around. They are not afraid of a fight or to put their life on the line and rarely back down from a challenge. They believe in their bones that they are here to defend those who cannot defend themselves. They are not happy to sit by and do nothing when they see something wrong happening. The Warrior usually has their own code which is not tied to a government; they will not take orders from just anybody. These codes are their way of life and are usually spiritual in nature.

They act first and think later or make decisions so quickly that they have not taken everything into consideration. They are prone to making mistakes and will more often than not have a mess to clean up and apologise for when they finally think about their actions. Some Warriors never do. They just keep constantly moving, hoping the past (and conscience) doesn't catch up with them.

Because they can assume too much at times as a result of being too quick to act or talk, they can find people around them frustrated or downright pissed off. It is a challenge for the Warrior to slow down, slow their bodies, minds, and mouths. If this archetype is spiritual, they will seek out mentorship to bring their mind, body, and spirit into alignment. Warriors like to be active with their bodies and enjoy being outside.

They can, like their Soldier brethren, be used in political games of power as pawns. The Warrior, however, will have to believe in what they are fighting for, whereas the Soldier will follow orders without question.

In Love and Relationships

The Knight of Swords needs to feel like they are on the same path as their significant other. They will seek out a partner who has similar beliefs and values. Out of all of the knights, they are the most likely to choose to be single.

This is because they never stop moving and are always on a mission. They can be impossible to keep up with.

They like to be intellectually stimulated or it is over before it begins. They cannot stand shallow, stupid, or bigoted people. If your mind isn't open, you are not worth their time. They love the idea of being in a relationship, just not the work. People are often attracted to this archetype as it is heavily romanticized in myth and culture, but they are rarely the kind of people who will stick it out with one person.

The Knight of Swords loves to be around people and are very social. They can tend to hop from social circle to social circle or have many groups of friends. They crave the new and exciting. The Knight of Swords is into fantasies and role playing in the bedroom. They like to keep things fresh in a relationship.

At Work and Career

Want something done? This is the tarot archetype who will get it done. Fast. It just may not be done with the most finesse. They welcome challenge in their work and if there is competition they are keen to win and be the best they can be.

The Knight of Swords needs to believe deeply in what they are achieving or helping get done or it is a no-go for them. They will simply find a better cause. They will research the company and the people that they are going to be working with before committing their energy to something.

They like to work somewhere where there is opportunity to advance. They are not going to stick around in any position if they feel unable to make change or make decisions. Stimulating and captivating projects or positions where they can consult with a number of different businesses are good for them.

The Knight of Swords may have a number of jobs or geographical locations in their lifetime, and if there is an opportunity to travel with work, it is even more appealing.

With the connection that this archetype has to their primal source and the discipline to train their body, many Warrior people will find they are natural athletes. This is a perfect outlet for their need to have camaraderie but also to oppose something, even if it is just their personal best.

Indicators that you are a Knight of Swords/Warrior archetype

- Role played the warrior as a child
- Drawn to/participated in martial arts in all forms
- Have tried to solve issues with fists before
- Quick to anger
- Have an underlying need to do something most of the time
- Enjoy being active
- Likes solo travel and adventure travel
- Seeks out spiritual mentorship when becoming the aware warrior

Knight of Swords Strengths

- Defends those who need it
- No hesitation when something needs doing
- First in the door
- Can inspire others to take action
- Daring
- Disciplined in what they value

Knight of Swords Shadow Side

- Bloodthirsty and aggressive
- Irrational
- Acts without thinking about the consequences
- Completely reactive
- Punishes without cause
- A pawn in someone else's game
- Vengeful

The Knight of Swords Archetype in a Tarot Reading

Identifying the tarot court as either an aspect of yourself playing out or another person is something that can trip up even the most experienced tarot

reader. When the Knight of Swords comes up in a tarot reading, be on the lookout for these behaviours as identifiers:

- A person who is always looking or ready for a fight. They check to see where the exits are when they walk into a room and never seem to fully let their guard down.

- The person who always seems to suffer from foot in mouth disease because they are notorious for speaking before they think and acting blindly.

- A person who is drawn to or actively participates in martial arts training. They may also like Kung-Fu Movies and collect decorative weapons and even may hunt as sport or to feed their family. Also the person in your life who likes paintball.

If the Knight of Swords comes up in a position that requires an outcome, action, or the next step forward, consider these actions as suggestions to move into the archetype's power:

- Ask yourself—Am I afraid to act? Making a choice and then acting on it can be really difficult if you are being blocked by fear. Working on the root cause of the fear can free yourself from indecision and stalemate.

- Take decisive action now; this is the time to act. No more sitting on the side lines.

- Ask—What would Wonder Woman do? Work with the character of the archetype and pop culture representations of that character to gain in-depth answers and options for moving forward.

THE PAGE OF SWORDS

Keywords

- Imagination
- Discovery
- Ideas
- Impulse

- Calculating
- Thinking
- Inquisitive
- Communication
- Questioning

Everyday Witch Tarot and Tarot Mucha

Astrology—No fixed astrological assignment.

The Page of Swords can be any of the air zodiac signs: Gemini, Aquarius, or Libra. They embody all of them. The Page of Swords has unlimited potential like all children.

Archetype—The Detective

The Detective is very alert and observant and knows when to speak and when to remain quietly in the background. While most things pass other people by, the Detective will notice and take note, making them people that you shouldn't underestimate. They understand a lot more than most people give them credit for. This is where a lot of their intelligence comes from. They are simply connected, observant, and aware. While they may not be as chatty as some of the other air court members, when they speak there is something of importance that they are trying to deliver/convey. The wise take note when this archetype speaks. They are always asking why, even if it is not verbalised.

They remind us that things do not need to be overly complicated. That is something that many of us do quite well—make things complicated. The Detective cuts right through that nonsense and gives us the simple, pure wisdom that was once lost.

This archetype sees patterns and symbols in places most people do not and is excellent at solving puzzles. They can be infuriating to watch crime movies with as they will gleefully tell you who done it and how they solved it before even the characters in the movie have had a chance. The idea of uncovering and discovering something hidden is intoxicating for this archetype. They never doubt their intuition and instinct and make their mind up about people quickly.

The Detective will be kept up at night trying to figure out a problem and will chase all leads until they can solve the current problem they are solving. Even if it is a crossword puzzle.

In Love and Relationships

The Page of Swords can have lofty ideals about relationships or even childish expectations. These are quickly shattered when experience of relationships happens to the Page of Swords.

Partners of this archetype can feel like they are an unsolved mystery or even being put under interrogation by their lover. It is because the Detective loves to see what makes people tick.

The Page of Swords is not one to commit easily. There is just too much out there to experience first. They are usually more concerned about their career and what is going on around them, than their relationships and putting work into them.

If they are in their shadow aspect, they can be distrustful of people at best and conniving back-stabbers at worst, who are going to find dirt on you and use it to their advantage.

At Work and Career

The Page of Swords is drawn to any profession or project where they get to explore knowledge and intellectual ideals. They want to put their mind to good use. If there isn't a problem to be solved or something to be found, the Page of Swords is not interested in the least.

They can work well in teams as long as they are allowed time and space to work in their own way. This archetype can become obsessive with hard to solve equations, problems, projects, or cases. This can drive the people around them bonkers as they disappear into the rabbit hole to solve their mystery.

Indicators that you are a Page of Swords/Detective archetype

- Puzzles are addicting
- Is usually the one asking the questions, not answering them
- Excellent at solving problems
- Extremely observant
- Can connect the dots that others don't see
- Enjoy work with lots of details
- Desire to understand motivations
- Silver tongued—can talk anything out of anyone

Page of Swords Strengths

- Intuitive
- Perceptive
- Can give lots of new perspectives
- A chameleon
- Full of questions
- Unwilling to settle for unfinished business

Page of Swords Shadow Side

- Ignorant
- Immature
- Can disappear in their head
- Blackmailer or back-stabber
- Can't be trusted and won't trust others
- Conniving

The Page of Swords Archetype in a Tarot Reading

Identifying the tarot court as either an aspect of yourself playing out or another person is something that can trip up even the most experienced tarot reader. When the Page of Swords comes up in a tarot reading, be on the lookout for these behaviours as identifiers:

- This person's favourite word is "why." They want to know what is going on and will likely question every detail in your plan before they get on board.
- This person can find anything, even if you think you were being clever and hid it. They are going to find their presents stashed in the back of your cupboard or those embarrassing photos you thought the internet forgot about.
- They notice ladybugs on leaves, patterns in the clouds, and pennies on the street and will spot the details that most people completely miss.

If the Page of Swords comes up in a position that requires an outcome, action, or the next step forward, consider these actions as suggestions to move into the archetype's power:

- Ask yourself—What inspires me? When we stimulate our minds with something inspirational it can allow us to relax, get a good dose of happy hormones, and often leads to incredible breakthroughs.
- Question everything, critically think, do your own research, get a second opinion. Now is not the time for blind faith.

- Ask—What would Sherlock Holmes do? Work with the character of the archetype and pop culture representations of that character to gain in-depth answers and options for moving forward.

EXERCISE: WHAT TAROT ARCHETYPE AM I?

PART 1—YOUR ARCHETYPE PILLARS

In this exercise we are going to explore what tarot archetypes you are made up of. What your personal tarot court looks like. You can be any of the court cards at any time, regardless of your age, gender identification, and colour of your hair. You could be the Casanova, Knight of Cups, in your romantic relationships, while at work you are the practical and structured King of Pentacles.

By doing this exercise, it will allow you to integrate your personality archetypes and shadow aspects, work on your strengths, reflect on how you can heal your relationships, become more successful at work, and release habits that no longer serve you. The court cards can also help you understand your development and challenges in your life.

To find out which of the tarot court members you are in the different areas or pillars, as they are called for this exercise, read through each of the indicators for each archetype. If you still find this difficult, work with a trusted friend or fellow tarot student or mentor and do the exercise together to give you some perspective.

For this exercise, you will need a deck of tarot cards and a notebook and pen.

1. Get one of your favourite tarot decks and separate the court cards from the rest of the deck.

2. Put the rest of the tarot deck aside for now.

3. Using the information given about the court card archetypes in the previous section, use the worksheet below to fill in your tarot archetypes.

Pillar One—Romantic Relationships

Your tarot court archetype

_____

Why did you select this card?

_____

_____

_____

Pillar Two—Your Family Relationships

Your tarot court archetype

_____

Why did you select this card?

_____

_____

_____

Pillar Three—Your Friendships

Your tarot court archetype

_____

Why did you select this card?

_____

_____

_____

Pillar Four—Your Work/Career

Your tarot court archetype

_____

Why did you select this card?

_____

_____

_____

Pillar Five—Your Health

Your tarot court archetype

_____

Why did you select this card?

_____

_____

_____

Pillar Six—Your Spiritual Archetype

Your tarot court archetype

_____

Why did you select this card?

_____

_____

_____

Pillar Seven—Your Inner Self

Your tarot court archetype

_____

Why did you select this card?

_____

_____

_____

Now that you have identified who you are in the pillars of your life, spend some time reflecting on each of the choices.

- Do you like the card?
- Are you surprised?
- Did you think you were going to be a different court card? If so which one?
- Do you like that you are represented as that court card?

This exercise can be a great way to see if there are roadblocks in your way to progressing to the place that you want to be.

If you find you have a lot of knights in all of the areas of your life, you may be experiencing a lot of change or taking too much action and not enough time to make good plans and set solid goals. If you have a lot of pages in your life, it may be time to grow up and take responsibility. Too many kings could indicate that you are fixed and rigid in your ways and could use a little fun and freedom. An abundance of queens could mean that you are nurturing and maybe need to release those well thought out ideas into the world and/or turn your energy inward to take care of yourself.

It can be beneficial to complete this exercise once every twelve months, because your tarot court archetypes will change as you grow, learn, break cycles, and complete relationships.

PART 2–TAROT ARCHETYPE ROADMAP READINGS

We are now going to expand on your archetypes and look at a roadmap for each pillar of your life. Using the seven pillars from part one, you will do a tarot reading for yourself, expanding and exploring the archetype more fully.

Note—Please complete part one of this exercise before you complete part two as the information you discovered in that exercise is used here.

If you find that you are the same tarot court card in more than one pillar of your life (which is completely fine and normal), use multiple tarot decks or place cards with the name of the court card in place of the card.

1. Take your seven court card archetype cards and lay them out in positions 1–7 like the following diagram.

2. Put the remaining court cards back into the deck and shuffle. Focus on the first pillar. When you feel ready, cut the deck and place one card on the left and two to the right of the archetype card.

3. Repeat step 2 for each of the 7 pillars, shuffling the deck while concentrating on each of the pillars.

4. Using some of the tips for interpreting the tarot reading provided, journal about your experience.

   • Are there any other court cards in the reading? Are they in the same elemental family?

   • Are there any major arcana cards in your reading? How does this impact your archetype? How does your archetype relate or deal with the major arcana energy?

   • Do any of the way forward/next step cards seem conflicting or backward? How does this feel?

Pillar One	8 Your strength in love	1 court card love archetype	9 Your challenge in love	10 The way forward Next step
Pillar Two	11 Your strength with family	2 court card family archetype	12 Your challenge with family	15 The way forward Next step
Pillar Three	14 Your strength with friends	3 court card friendship archetype	15 Your challenge with friends	16 The way forward Next step
Pillar Four	17 Your strength in work	4 court card work archetype	18 Your challenge in work	19 The way forward Next step
Pillar Five	20 Your strength in health	5 court card health archetype	21 Your challenge in health	22 The way forward Next step
Pillar Six	23 Your strength in spirituality	6 court card spiritual archetype	24 Your challenge in spirituality	25 The way forward Next step
Pillar Seven	26 Your inner self strength	7 court card inner strength archetype	27 Your inner self challenge	28 The way forward Next step

~ Nine ~
TAROT COURT LOVE CONNECTIONS

Now we are going to explore in depth how the tarot court card archetypes act in love, relationships, and lust. You will discover information about how the archetypes court, fall in love, and act in a relationship. When reading the tarot for prediction, something that tarot readers are asked frequently is to tell their querent about the person they will end up marrying or who their soulmate is. I use the court cards a lot when reading the cards in this manner. They can tell me and my clients about their personality in a relationship, what they are likely to respond to, and how to help them when they are dealing with difficult things in their lives.

You can use the information below to help yourself and/or your tarot clients find love and what to be on the lookout for in regards to behaviours and actions.

We can be a layer of the tarot court as well and hold different court card positions for different relationships. The way we interact with our siblings is different to the way we interact with our parents. The relationship we have with our work colleagues is not the same as an intimate relationship, although many people mix the two. In this chapter, we are going to focus on how the tarot court card archetypes move through the stages of romantic love, as these are the most powerful, frustrating, transforming, and intoxicating relationships we experience in our lifetime.

Love evolves and changes just as we do, and we will shift and change from different archetypes of the tarot court in different relationships and with time. It is completely normal for people to experience more than one of these love archetypes throughout their lives. You may see reflections of your past self in a number of these archetypes.

When taking this information into consideration, please be aware that every person is different and every relationship is different. The pairings in the charts as well as their love and relationships traits are shared as a way to help you understand your relationships and the people you love better. They are not hard-and-fast rules as to who you should date, marry, or blow off.

When your querent is seeking information about a future romantic partner and a court card comes up, you can use the information below to help your client understand their potential lover. It will also help the tarot reader to demystify these cards so you can give clear and specific information to your clients.

When the court card comes up in a relationship reading in a position of opposition or challenge or is reversed, you may find that the behaviours that are being shown are in the shadow or sadness and grief areas of the information given in each court card meaning. This information can help people get themselves (if they are reading for themselves) or their querent's loved one back into alignment by understanding their behaviour and fostering the more positive aspects of the archetypes. This is in no way to excuse abusive behaviour of any kind, and professional help should be sought out if there is serious concern for someone's health or safety.

Adding your own intuitive and learned meanings on top of this can allow you to build your own set of meanings for the court cards in love readings.

THE KING OF CUPS–HADES– THE LORD OF THE UNDERWORLD

When courting a relationship, this archetype will read books of philosophy and classic literature to be seen as a deep individual. They will quote famous lines from books and leave said books laying around so you will see that they have read them. If they are serious in courting you, they will find out what your favourite author or poet is and be doing their homework. If the King of Cups has their desires locked on you, you will know it.

The King of Cups will use mystery and silence as a way to attract people to them. They will also have a reputation, good or bad, within their circle, but they have no interest in validating the truth or the falseness of their reputation. They want you to find out on your own whether or not it is true. They are not shy in looking people in the eye to create a connection, which can be too intense for some.

Steampunk Tarot and Everyday Witch Tarot

They can come across as distant and snobbish, but this is usually a front and a way to protect themselves from being hurt or for people to see that they have a huge heart and fall deeply in love when they find a connection they want to keep.

Hades can be an exceptionally tentative lover who enjoys giving sexual pleasure as much as receiving, and sex is usually an extension of love for this archetype.

If they are in their shadow aspect, they are more likely to be the kind of lover who keeps people on a string so that there is always someone who will come and comfort them when they need their fill. They also know exactly what they are doing with their sexual energy. This archetype in their shadow aspect can also be more susceptible to having way too much dependence on alcohol or other addictive substances and this will jeopardise the relationships that they are in.

In a committed loving relationship, they are present, protective, and will put the people that they consider family at the forefront of their minds.

When fighting in a relationship and dealing with sadness and or grief, the King of Cups will become one moody, broody king. They are most likely to need a lot of time alone to process their feelings and will not react kindly to people pushing them to talk about it. To support a King of Cups during this time is to acknowledge that you understand their need for space but that you will be there when they are ready to talk.

Example of a Perfect Love Connection for the King of Cups

- The Knight of Pentacles—The Soldier—Nothing like a steady, strong, loyal Knight of Pentacles to be there through the King of Cups's emotional storms. The King of Cups is also likely to awaken the sexual life of the Knight of Pentacles, which serves this partnership well. They can both tend to be serious, but they also want a deeper relationship, which suits them both just fine.

Example of a Troubled Love Connection for the King of Cups

- Queen of Cups—The Mystic—These two connect deeply on an emotional and sexual level, but when the relationship starts to have problems, their fights can be epic with both emotionally separating from each other. If they have strong communication skills, they can make it work, but they also need a hefty amount of emotional intelligence to navigate this relationship long-term.

THE QUEEN OF CUPS—THE MYSTIC

The Queen of Cups loves being romanced, but due to past experiences with being judged and persecuted for their intuitive and psychic talents (even if this was not in this lifetime), they may not divulge their gifts to the person they are dating straight away. It is not that they want to deceive the other person, they just need to know that they are in a safe place before they fully open up. This archetype may come across as a little hot and cold or shy at times, but they do like to be courted. Rejection is this court card's Achilles' heel, so they will want to know how the other person is feeling before they open up and start to show who they are authentically. They will watch how the person they are dating reacts in situations where kindness is needed and will see if they have any energetic sensitivities themselves. If they find someone who is able to give them energetic backup, they will be extremely happy.

Bad Bitches Tarot and Tarot Mucha

As a lover the Mystic will know the other person's pleasure zones and desires without being told. They know when to stop and when to keep going. Being in sync with their lover rocks both of their socks. They want you to show them through touch how much you appreciate them. They can tend to overgive so if you are a partner of a Mystic, make sure you are giving as much as you are receiving.

If the Mystic is in their shadow in a relationship, they will become very emotionally insecure, which can come across as jealousy. They may fish for constant reassurance that the person they love loves them back. It doesn't help that the Mystic is going to pick up on their partner's attraction to other people, even if it is just a passing interest.

When the Queen of Cups is in a committed relationship, they are extremely compassionate. They do tend to move quickly in their relationships, forgetting to enjoy and take their time with dating. They are all in or not in at all. When they are secure in their relationships, they would rather stay at home entertaining than be around strangers.

During a fight, the Mystic will shut down and become a brick wall. They will give nothing and refuse to tell others why they are upset. If they bottle up their emotions too much, they are likely to become overwhelmed and cry tears of frustration, but be unable to express exactly why they are upset.

When dealing with sadness and grief, they are likely to hide away in isolation and may not be able to handle the needs of others while grieving. They will need to take care of their emotional bodies and energetic hygiene when they are in a place of grief, as they will find they will get emotionally overwhelmed quickly.

Example of a Perfect Love Connection for the Queen of Cups

- The Queen of Cups—The Mystic—Mystics are naturally attracted to each other. A fellow Mystic can actually help with bringing a mirror into this person's life. They will allow them safe space to be who they really are and also communicate on levels that most people are unable to in their relationships. This relationship will need to have a good group of friends to keep them grounded and social.

Example of a Troubled Love Connection for the Queen of Cups

- Knight of Swords—The Warrior—This archetype will not be emotionally and physically available in the way that the Mystic needs. They will put everything and everyone else in front of their relationship without understanding that they are doing it. The Warrior will put their own Warrior/spiritual journey before any relationship, leaving the Mystic feeling rejected and neglected.

THE KNIGHT OF CUPS—THE ROMANTIC

Hold on to your bedpost! Here comes the lover of all lovers. When it comes to courting, this is the archetype that makes the rules (usually as they go and always to suit themselves) and runs the game. The bigger the challenge in the conquest the better. They know they are hot and they have the reputation and trail of broken hearts behind them to prove it. While you know that this person has their well-earned reputation, they will make you feel as though you are the exception to the rule because they are just so into whoever they are dating. They love love, so they are going to ensure that you are having an amazing time when you are with them. It is an amazing feeling being with a Cassanova while you are their desire.

Tarot Mucha and Steampunk Tarot

The Romantic is a wonderful lover not only because they have had a lot of experience, but because they view lovemaking as an art and they want to live up to their street cred. They are playful when you need picking up, sexy, slow, and sensual when you need some love magic in your life, and kinky when things need spicing up. If you are with a Romantic and they are not an aware person or are dwelling in their shadow side, they can think they are incredible in bed but are actually terrible. They will think that their natural talents are enough to ensure they are a sure bet in bed when it takes so much more.

The shadow Knight of Cups is all about racking up the numbers and usually filling the void in their life by being with people because being alone is unbearable and so is the thought of being in a committed relationship. Classic woo them, love them, use them, lose them. They will be the type to have little black books. They have multiple partners at a time without anyone knowing that is the case, and will run at the first sign of trouble or commitment. They have unrealistic expectations about what love is because they ultimately need to learn to love themselves.

Commitment and the die hard romantic rarely go together. They are more likely to be committed to themselves and the idea that they are meant to be wild and free to love who they can, while they can. Some people are just not meant to be in monogamous relationships. This does come with a hefty amount of judgement from more traditional archetypes, but for some people there is more danger in trying to be someone they are not rather than being alone. It is more likely that, if you are a Romantic, your primary love archetype will change if and when you are ready to commit.

When faced with a fight with a lover, this archetype tends to get over it pretty quickly and will exit as fast as they can. Why spend your time fighting instead of loving? When the person that they are with wants to fight they will try to solve the fight with their hottest moves. What is the point in fighting if you can't have amazing make up sex?

The Romantic is likely to dive right into being a broody artist when they are dealing with grief and sadness. They will listen to music that matches their mood, explore different artistic avenues, and try to make themselves feel better through lovemaking. They will want other people to witness and validate their sadness.

Example of a Perfect Love Connection for the Knight of Cups

- The Page of Wands—Peter Pan—This is a perfect match for the time they will spend together, but it still doesn't mean there will be wedding bells. They will just have a really hot, fun, incredible time together, and both archetypes really don't like things getting too serious or heavy, so it works out well for both of them.

Example of a Troubled Love Connection for the Knight of Cups

- The King of Swords—The Scientist—This archetype simply has no time for the Romantic's game. They are more likely to kill each other if they try to make a relationship work. This doesn't mean that the Romantic won't try to pull the moves on a powerful executive archetype like the Scientist. It just won't stick, as the Scientist will get very bored and see through them.

THE PAGE OF CUPS–THE EMPATH

The Empath is a dating genius because they know within seconds of meeting someone if they have a future with them. This can come across to others as being way too picky, but they just don't see the advantage in letting the wrong person get too close to them. The other side to this incredible people radar is that they find it hard to find someone they will open up to. If they feel that the person they are dating is hiding too much or isn't going to be understanding of their empathic gifts, they will not pursue that relationship. Small, thoughtful gestures are a way into this archetype's heart.

Empaths can find expressing their own true emotions difficult if they have not worked on developing and protecting their gifts. At times they may be unsure what emotions and needs are actually their own and what is something that they are picking up on from someone else.

As lovers, Empaths will want to go out of their way to make their partners happy and satisfied. If they have not done any work on their energetic and emotional intelligence, they may find it hard to receive pleasure and love, hiding by being of service to others instead.

If the Page of Cups is operating in a shadow aspect, they can be incredibly immature. They will blame everyone else for their emotions and feelings.

When things start to go wrong in a relationship, they will rarely be able to take it in a way that isn't highly emotional. They want to place the blame somewhere else and make the other person feel as bad as they do.

Bad Bitches Tarot and Everyday Witch Tarot

Empaths do not tend to be single for long, or if they are, they will have a co-dependent, platonic relationship somewhere in their lives. They want to have the emotional security that being with someone brings. If they are with a balanced partner, their gifts will flourish and they will find that being in a relationship sees them at the height of their creative selves. Empaths do need and like their own space and will often need something like a shed, art room, yoga room, or meditation space in their home to come back to and reset from all of the energy that they pick up.

Fighting is not really their modus operandi. Empaths will hold onto all of their pain, especially if they are stressed and don't have the time to sort through how they are really feeling. They will break down or blow up when it all becomes too much. They can be triggering to their partners as they will hold the energy that is being sent their way. It is important for Empaths to learn how to ground and protect their own personal energy and not to become relationship punching bags.

Not many other tarot court archetypes experience grief and sadness like the Empath. It can hit them like a ton of bricks. A lot of Empaths have taken on their loved ones' pains from a young age, trying to ease the suffering of those around them. This can continue into their relationships, and many Empaths may not be aware that they even do this. Processing grief is one of this archetype's major life lessons, so it is something they are always working on.

Example of a Perfect Love Connection for the Page of Cups

- The Knight of Pentacles—The Soldier—This loyal and grounded individual is a perfect match for the Empath. They are solid and calm in crisis situations and are understanding when the Empath needs space. They will likely grow with each other as well.

Example of a Troubled Love Connection for the Page of Cups

- The King of Cups—Hades—This connection is usually way too much for the Empath who will be completely overwhelmed with the King's need to keep pushing and digging on pain points. These two connections are better as friends or student/mentor.

THE KING OF PENTACLES—THE MANAGER

This archetype in love wants to be in control and will be the one who sets the tone and drives the relationship forward. They will make the plans for your date, will be on time and will expect that their date be on time as well. They are more than happy to shower the person they are dating with gifts, especially as words are not their strongest point. This is also how you show this archetype that you are interested in them. Words mean very little to them in relationships—time and action mean more. Their body language will tell you a lot about how they feel about the prospect of their relationship.

As a lover, the Manager will take the lead and be the more dominant one in the bedroom. Giving them feedback on how they can be a more attentive lover may be tricky as they are not used to being coached in that way. They will not hesitate to make the first move if they are interested in taking the next step to make the relationship intimate.

Everyday Witch Tarot and Triple Goddess Tarot

If the Manager is in the shadow aspect, they can be very hard to re-move from your life. They can become a control freak or jealous, track your phone, not want you to go out without them, and even show stalker tenden-cies. They are just not sure what is too much and when to back off. They will likely want to know where you are at all times and what you are doing. It can be creepy.

In a committed relationship, this tarot archetype will likely throw money at any issue that comes up. If you are mad at them, they will buy you a gift. If they forgot a meaningful date, you are likely to get a international holiday out of it. They simply do not want to have to deal with the emotional on-slaught or even have to admit they were wrong, so this is the easiest thing to do. Avoiding an argument is best in their books. On the positive side, this person will make sure that their family is well taken care of. There is always money to pay the bills and have luxuries, and they fit the provider mold well.

When dealing with grief and sorrow, the King of Pentacles is better at helping others through their hard times rather than dealing with their own emotions. They will be practical, as this is how they deal with things. If there is nothing that they can change, they will simply accept it and try to move on without really grieving. They are not very good at showing most people their vulnerabilities. If you are with this tarot court archetype and they open up to you, know that this is very rare indeed.

Example of a Perfect Love Connection for the King of Pentacles
- The Queen of Pentacles—The Healer—Another grounded and earthy soul, this partnership can go the distance as long as the Healer is happy to let the Manager lead in the relationship.

Example of a Troubled Love Connection for the King of Pentacles
- The Queen of Swords—The Judge—Fighting would consume most of this relationship with both being unwilling to relent. The Judge won't allow the Manager to get away with their BS or avoidance tactics, and the Manager won't take the confrontation and questioning well.

THE QUEEN OF PENTACLES–THE HEALER

So many people will find the Healer attractive because of the incredible space they provide for people. When they are courting someone, they will instantly have the other person feeling welcomed and valued. They seem to always have time to help others, especially those they care about. The Healer does not like shallow people or flighty people. If you find yourself courting the Healer, don't play games. Be upfront and show integrity with them. (This can be said for all relationships, really, but this archetype will not suffer any BS.) If you are looking for gifts for this tarot archetype, know that they would prefer a pretty crystal or river stone you found over an expensive diamond.

As a lover they may not be the most kinky in bed, but they will make sure that their partner is satisfied before they are. As a healer, sex is a healing and sacred art to them, so they take this part of their relationship very seriously. This archetype can be a perfect tantric sexual healer and help people unlock and reawaken lost intimacy, not to mention be a powerhouse when it comes to the ultimate climax.

Bad Bitches Tarot and Tarot Mucha

If the Healer is unhappy, they will likely make their entire household unhappy too. They will want to be heard and validated before they are willing to lift the dark cloud they hold over everyone. They can hold onto grudges like it is a profession and will fight until they feel satisfied regardless of how it is affecting everyone else involved. Selfish is definitely a word they may hear from exes.

This tarot archetype loves a committed relationship and often does much better in one than out of one or just casually dating. They adore waking up next to the same person. They love creating or carrying on family traditions and caring for others. They will make their home a truly beautiful space.

When they are fighting they can be very passive aggressive and unable to see from the other person's point of view. Their steam runs out quickly, however, as fighting physically affects them, and they are likely to get headaches or make themselves sick if they stay in a state of distress for too long.

When dealing with sadness and grief, the Healer may hide away in their bed, unable to move or really care about much while they process their emotions. They will get up and go through the motions if someone else needs them, but they won't really be engaged. As a healer they tend to everyone else's pain first. This can lead to long term sickness or exhaustion if they do not take their self-care seriously.

Example of a Perfect Love Connection for the Queen of Pentacles

- The King of Cups—Hades—These two will be so in sync that they will likely annoy the crap out of all of their friends. They love deep conversation and crave intimate time together. If they are working from an awakened, conscious space, this couple can help other couples and society at large.

Example of a Troubled Love Connection for the Queen of Pentacles

- The Queen of Wands—The Performer—They will be forever chasing this person. They will try to serve this person and relationship, giving everything but finding themselves lost and drained.

THE KNIGHT OF PENTACLES–THE SOLDIER

If you are ever courted by the Soldier, know that this person has probably admired you from afar for a long time. They have painstakingly gone over every word they will say to you and the multiple roads the conversation may go down before they let their feelings be known. This tarot archetype will also rather be friends with their partners first. They want to know them well. Due to their conservative nature, large romantic gestures are rare. You may not know they are even flirting with you. They are all about actions. This is how you know how they feel. They will be there for you and do what they say they are going to do.

As a lover, the Soldier may find it hard to accept pleasure and deep love to begin with. It can take some understanding and patience, but when they feel safe they will begin to let go of their need to control themselves at all times. They are very self-critical, so believing they are worth all of the good things in a relationship can be hard to accept. Things may get a little mechanical in bed with this archetype. They like what they like and aren't really into sexy surprises, so make sure you don't suggest any naughty gifts to them at the last minute in the bedroom.

Everyday Witch Tarot and Steampunk Tarot

The Soldier in the shadow aspect can completely check out. They will simply not be present at all. They will do what they have to but be a million miles away. They will put their personal duty and purpose before their relationship. They can also become a very lazy lover, partner, and parent and let things slip too much.

In a committed relationship, even if things are unhealthy or flat out bad, they are likely to stick it out longer than they should because they have such a deep belief in loyalty. They will take just about anything from someone they love—good or bad. This archetype needs commitment, steadiness, and dependability and in return will give all of those things back to the person they are with. Long-term relationships are often their core desire.

This archetype will immediately go into defensive mode when they are fighting. This can be a good thing if you need someone to have your back, but can be very difficult to navigate if they are fighting against you. It can be hard for them to really hear the other person. The Soldier actually likes fighting, and if they are not getting their challenge elsewhere, such as at work or recreationally, they can tend to pick fights at home. If you are with this archetype and find that fights are constant, sign them up for rugby or a contact sport; it may help.

Example of a Perfect Love Connection for the Knight of Pentacles

- The Knight of Pentacles—The Soldier—There is something about being with someone who has been through similar experiences and has the same codes of loyalty for this archetype. They do well with like minded souls.

Example of a Troubled Love Connection for the Knight of Pentacles

- The Page of Wands—Peter Pan—While the Soldier may find the fun and lightheartedness of Peter Pan attractive, and they may very well want to save them from themselves. The desire fades when they realise there is not much substance there for them to build a solid foundation on.

THE PAGE OF PENTACLES—THE NATURALIST

The Naturalist will fall in love with you through your pet and you will likely meet at a dog park or volunteering at an animal shelter. If you don't like pets, animals, and nature, then don't waste your time with this person. You have to be willing to share this person with their animals. When dating, the Naturalist will want to be doing fun activities or even just walking or moving. It centres their energy. Things like walking in nature, hiking, or going to the beach are good ideas for dates.

If you are looking to be intimate with the Naturalist, I hope you like nookie outdoors. They do. They will enjoy making love under the stars on a camping trip, on a hiking trail, and anywhere they may get away with it. This archetype, apart from their nature sexual fantasies, can get into habits of lovemaking very quickly, and routines tend to stick. It is not to say that sex with them will be bad, it will just be very routine if things are not kept spicy by you both.

Steampunk Tarot and Tarot Mucha

Loving the Naturalist can be extremely frustrating if they are in their shadow. They aren't likely to want to do much and people often fall in love with their potential, which is rarely met. Even more frustrating is that they won't be very aware, being a bit of a snob about it or finding lots of excuses as to why the timing is not right.

In a committed relationship, they are stable, solid, and predictable. You always know what you are getting with this person, which for some people is not a bad thing at all. They will love being in a relationship as long as their partner loves animals and doesn't mind the fact that their house is a menagerie. Unless they work professionally with animals, they are unlikely to a hold a career that is going to light the world on fire.

When the Naturalist is fighting with their loved one, they will be very childish and often act like a wounded animal, turning on the doe eyes and looking at their partner with a "please don't yell at me" face. Tantrums are pretty standard when things are not going their way as they are not very good at articulating negative feelings.

When they are experiencing grief and sadness, their loyal and trusty pets will be a huge comfort to them. They will be more affected when an animal passes away than most people they know. Becoming reclusive and non-verbal is a common way for this archetype to behave when suffering.

Example of a Perfect Love Connection for the Page of Pentacles

- The Page of Cups—The Empath—This couple may be a little insular or seemingly codependent to the outside world, but they compliment each other so well that the relationship can really bloom. But they must also maintain some outside friends and individual passion projects.

Example of a Troubled Love Connection for the Page of Pentacles

- The King of Swords—The Scientist—The Scientist will simply be too cold and withdrawn for the Naturalist to be able to be with them. While they both love the natural world and have that in common, they come at it from a very different place and that would be a breaking factor for their relationship.

THE KING OF WANDS—THE ENTREPRENEUR

The Entrepreneur is usually well known in their circles for being a bit of a showboat and player. However, they are extremely fun to date because they will show you things you have never seen before and give you experiences that are usually only for VIPs. They will take you backstage to concerts or an exclusive restaurant. They are well connected and will not mind showing you that. This tarot archetype loves the chase. In fact, they will love the chase more than the relationship, so if you are with this person, planning surprises and adventures will never go unnoticed or unappreciated.

As a lover, they covet pleasure, affection, and attention. They love to receive these things and will want to be shown that they are appreciated. So don't be shy or quiet in bed with this one. If their needs are being met, they can also be generous at giving. If not, they will be selfish. Find out how they like to be loved. Underneath all of the posing, they ultimately want to please and be praised. They will also be okay with handing over the reins of control in the bedroom, as every other area of their lives needs careful personal managing.

Tarot Mucha and Bad Bitches Tarot

If the Entrepreneur is operating out of their shadow side in a relationship, they will have no issues using people to get what they want. They hold very high expectations of the people they are with and no one ever lives up to them. They are prone to making reckless decisions that leave them single because they lead and make decisions impulsively. There is a reason they work for themselves after all.

The Entrepreneur will likely have more than one serious committed relationship in their lives. They are more committed to themselves and their work than other people. They will look for someone who is also in a position of influence in their work and will want them to have their backs and help them take on the world.

When in a fight, they love to be the centre of attention, so expect a lot of hot air and the occasional air projectile. They are used to getting their own way and because of this have no problems starting fights. At times their volcanic disposition is quickly forgotten, but everyone else around them is left to pick up the pieces.

When they experience sadness and grief, they will just bury themselves in their work. They will take to humanitarian and charity work, championing a cause that has touched them personally. They are vocal about helping because they want to be seen.

Example of a Perfect Love Connection for the King of Wands

• The Queen of Wands—The Performer—One wants to take on the world in a business way and the other wants the world to really see them. They will love the shared influence and limelight that being together brings. They don't want the same kind of attention, so they will work together well as a couple.

Example of a Troubled Love Connection for the King of Wands

• The King of Pentacles—The Manager—You know the saying, oil and water don't mix and this is a living example of it. One will crave structure and stability and the other will make rash decisions without a second thought about their relationship.

THE QUEEN OF WANDS–THE PERFORMER

When the performer is courting someone, they will make them feel like they are the only person in the room and the world. They are charismatic and the person they are dating is often not quite sure how they landed such a fabulous partner to begin with. Because the performer likes an audience they will not be shy about letting a person know they are interested and will expect a lot of attention back. They will let you know they want to be chased and coveted like the prize they know they are. Once they have you on their radar, they rarely don't get what they want.

As a lover, the performer is warm, extroverted, and sexy. They are enthusiastic about pleasure and will bring an element of their archetypal namesake to the bedroom. They will want the perfect stage set and the environment to be supportive of an award-winning performance. This doesn't mean they will want to be the one in the lead in the bedroom. This may be one of the rare areas where they will play a more supportive role.

Everyday Witch Tarot and Tarot Mucha

If the performer in a relationship is acting out of their shadow, then expect a whole lot of diva behaviour. Heaven forbid you forget a birthday or anniversary. You will never hear the end of it. This tarot archetype can also be the poster child for jealous behaviour and can be capable of some very extreme things when they feel unseen, threatened, or locked out in a relationship.

If you do not like the limelight, then this may not be the right person for you to covet a long-term relationship with. While they may be used to being the centre of attention and being out mingling, that kind of behaviour is not for everyone and the performer will not give up their art for anyone. Not because they are selfish, but because it is who they are. They will want their partner to pay attention to what is going on in their lives, even if you have been with them a long time. If they have a new hairstyle or tattoo, show them you have noticed. They often want to be seen in a certain way and praise means a lot to them, so show that you are proud to be such an important part of their lives.

If you ever get into a fight with the Queen of Wands, I hope you know how to run and duck for cover, because they are one heck of a thunderstorm when they feel backed into a corner. Walking away from them is not a good idea. They will demand that they are listened to and they still want your attention even if they are pissed. The root cause of fighting can often be due to jealousy, even if there is no cause for it at all.

When the performer is dealing with sadness and grief, they can be found racking up their credit cards to make themselves feel better or flirting with people outside of their relationship and getting into public displays of emotional outbursts. They can either find some of their best artistic work in this space or it can be something that derails them from their creative genius.

Example of a Perfect Love Connection for the Queen of Wands

- The Queen of Swords—The Judge—The performer will appreciate being with someone who doesn't crave the spotlight. The judge is able to keep up with the performer, keep them honest and grounded, and call them out when they are being too much of a diva.

Example of a Troubled Love Connection for the Queen of Wands

- The King of Cups—Hades—While they will want to tear each others clothes off in public when their passion can't wait, this connection can get dark quickly. Hades will get bored of whatever scene the performer is in and likely manipulate everyone in it, making the relationship miserable and unhealthy.

KNIGHT OF WANDS—THE ADVENTURER

No one can tell a story quite like this tarot archetype because they have seen and experienced so much and they are enchanting and a little dangerous because of it. Their passports are full of stamps and their living spaces are wall to wall of eye-dropping photos of exotic places. They will be more than happy to romance you with everything that they have. They are confident and self-reliant, and will take you on incredible adventures when you are together.

Steampunk Tarot and Bad Bitches Tarot

There is nothing that this lover won't do in bed—fuzzy handcuffs, sex swings, or sex clubs. They are up for just about anything, chasing a new experience because everything is an adventure. You may not always get to see this lover, but they do love sending romantic messages and like the idea of having someone waiting for them when they get home. They are restless in love as well as in life.

This tarot archetype in their shadow will have a lover in every port, city, and country. They will purposefully get into shitty relationships that they know are doomed to fail because the drama and the story of them getting out of it will be worth it. They are likely to run away from relationships, leaving a trail of broken hearts and people wondering what they did wrong.

They will have no problems projecting their fear onto the other person and making them take the fall for the relationship ending. It will make them feel better about it at least.

Commitment and this archetype do not go and in hand. So while they are so good with people and love being around people in general, they may not ever be able to shake the need for new places and experiences. If you are into long distance, open relationships, and experimentation, then it may work.

This archetype loves to fight and challenge their partners, which can get really draining quickly. When fighting with a loved one, they will pace like a caged animal. If you want to talk things out with your Adventurer partner, then go for a walk or drive with them and talk. They are excellent solo travellers, but travelling with a significant other may just be their undoing as they will find it hard to make space for the other person; their desire for experience and adventure will override their partner duties and they can come across as selfish and inconsiderate with their choices.

When this tarot archetype is dealing with sadness and grief, they will get into whatever escapism they are currently into, like gaming, booze, porn, gambling, or sex, and do it excessively as a coping mechanism. That is if they are simply unable to get on a plane and try running away from their pain.

Example of a Perfect Love Connection for the Knight of Wands

- The King of Wands—The Entrepreneur—Both of these archetypes love freedom and have enough going on in their own lives that they are secure with the other doing what they please for the most part. They will have travel, money, and sex in common and it will keep things moving along for a long while.

Example of a Troubled Love Connection for the Knight of Wands

- The Queen of Cups—The Mystic—The Adventurer will want to be experiencing everything and be all over the place and the Mystic would much rather be in their sacred space that feels like home. The Mystic also knows what is going to undo their relationship well before it happens and avoids these people rather than get their heart broken.

THE PAGE OF WANDS—PETER PAN

This is such a playful tarot archetype that you cannot help but have an amazing time when you are dating one. Your dates will be filled with playful activities, retro sports, nostalgic movies, and music, and you will be loving every moment. They can, however, tend to be a little flaky, but they are so charming most people will let them get away with a certain amount of it. They will pursue you adoringly and with a lot of energy. They tend to talk a good game but have very little real world experience to back it up.

Everyday Witch Tarot and Steampunk Tarot

In the bedroom, games and role play are a big turn-on, as is sex in public places and anywhere where there is a risk of getting caught in the act. They will happily accept a dare and will want other people to be as adventurous as they are. Unfortunately they don't always know when it becomes dangerous to keep pushing the envelope because they won't stop trying to up the stakes.

When in a relationship and in their shadow, they will be all about lying and cheating, often to the extreme where it will leave a number of people feeling as though they have been played. They won't understand why what they are doing is unacceptable and will likely shrug it off and keep on doing what they want. They can be very childish, immature, and sometimes down-right mean.

If they ever do get into a committed relationship, it probably won't be the first or last one in their lives. They will often have more than one child with different people and have a few weddings in their lifetimes. If they ever really do settle down, it won't be until they are good and ready and when they are middle-aged. When they are with someone they truly love, they will really be with them, They just don't often have the staying power, as relationships are hard work and they are not into anything that involves hard work.

When fighting in a relationship, they will act like children with tantrums, name calling, and avoidance, and they won't apologise for the things they have done wrong. If they do say sorry, they are unlikely to really mean it and will do it again the next time. In the extreme, they can be a bully in their re-lationship and really go for the other person's weak spots. Winning the fight is worth destroying the other person in their minds.

When dealing with sadness and grief, they will storm off and pout and won't want to deal with it in a mature manner. They will want everyone else to make them feel better. They will also want to be taken care of. They won't have an issue expressing that they are hurt. They just don't have any tact about how they go about it.

Example of a Perfect Love Connection for the Page of Wands

- The Page of Wands—Peter Pan—They may drive everyone one else to distraction with their inability to grow up and take control of their lives, but their lives together with never be dull.

Example of a Troubled Love Connection for the Page of Wands

- The King of Wands—The Entrepreneur—The mature person in this relationship is going to feel like they are always chastising a small child and will get sick of it very quickly, regardless of Peter Pan's charm and ability to keep the other feeling young.

THE KING OF SWORDS—THE SCIENTIST/SPECIALIST

If you are ever interested in romantically pursuing this tarot archetype, you are going to have to chase them or make it painfully obvious that you are interested in them, as flirting and subtle suggestions to ask you out will likely go over their heads. The Scientist finds intelligence very sexy, but will still want to be smarter than the person they are dating, or at least work in a different field so they can still be seen as the top of their game. Socially, if you ever get this person out from behind their chosen work desk, they may not take you to the most conventional dating destinations, but if you are a perfect match for them, you are going to find their date of stargazing at an observatory completely mind blowing.

Tarot Mucha and Bad Bitches Tarot

As a lover, expect this archetype to have read up on the subject. Assuming they have a sex drive, most of their energy may be spent trying to finish their latest project or cure a rare disease. They want to please and be a good lover at least partially because they don't like failing at anything. They may not be the kind of lover to write poems or come through with a lot of romantic gestures, but they are very good between the sheets. However, they can seem very on or off. There isn't an in-between when it comes to their interest in a person or in getting down.

If the Scientist is in a relationship and acting out of their shadow, they will want to control their partner. They will likely want to control all aspects of their life together too, such as not sharing information or telling the truth about their finances and having control over their assets. They can be the kind of partner who verbally abuses or manipulates and puts down their partner in public. Shutting their loved ones out is also a shadow move for this archetype.

When in a committed relationship with this person, work needs to be done to keep the emotional connection alive. They honestly believe that they know what is right and best for their partner and, if they are in a position of influence at work, what is best for the world. While they are fair and loyal partners and good providers, they will also want to lead the relationship and make most of the large decisions on behalf of the family, such as what schools your children will attend.

This is an archetype that rarely has time to fight with their partner. When they do step up to argue, they will pull out examples of something that happened years ago down to the last details, so be prepared to fight with someone who remembers everything. They can be extremely stubborn and lack empathy, so getting them to see your side of the fight can be tough.

When dealing with sadness and grief the Scientist will just bury themselves in work, religion, spirituality, or research, but that is not going to really get them anywhere. They can become detached from the situation and the world and are not very good at providing support to those around them that may be looking for it, opting instead for isolation from everyone and everything.

Example of a Perfect Love Connection for the King of Swords

- The Queen of Swords—The Judge—Both of these people find intelligence extremely attractive and it is lucky that between them they have enough to sink a ship. They will be able to keep up with each other and challenge each other well. They will also be a pretty balanced relationship, with both parties being able to come to things rationally.

Example of a Troubled Love Connection for the King of Swords

- The Page of Wands—Peter Pan—The Scientist will find this personality the most annoying thing on the planet and Peter Pan will just want to poke the old stick in the mud all the time for fun. Best to leave these two to better suited lovers.

THE QUEEN OF SWORDS—THE JUDGE

If this tarot archetype is interested in you, they will find a way to cross paths with you. If at all possible, they will orchestrate an opportunity for you to see them working, as it is a great turn-on for them and they know they shine at work. They may appear nonchalant about your attention but actually care deeply about what you think. The Judge will love to take you to social and charity events that they are interested and believe in. A good way to lock this person down is to get along with their friends, quickly.

The Judge as a lover will be pretty upfront about what they like and what they don't like in the bedroom, what you need to do, and for how long. They like dirty talk—and don't be surprised if they are a bit kinky in bed. This is a person who likes to be in a relationship and will also want their sex lives to be fantastic, interesting, and stimulating.

There are three words that describe this person if they are in a relationship and acting out of their shadow side: cold, manipulative, and cruel. They cannot only emotionally manipulate you like a professional, but will screw with your head in the process. If they are a really nasty piece of work, they will try to cut you off from your family and friends so they have total control over you.

In a committed relationship that is healthy, they are very loyal and if you break their trust, there is no going back. Their relationships become a large focus of their lives. They like to keep any issues they may have in the relationship a secret in order to maintain appearances. Being a little all-or-nothing, they will want to know that the person they are in a long-term relationship with is in it for the long haul.

Everyday Witch Tarot and Triple Goddess Tarot

When fighting, the Judge is a force of nature. You may want to think long and hard before fighting with this one because you are going to go up against someone who has debating in their DNA. They can cut through people with their words and will keep calm and collected while their hail of word bullets sends the other person into a complete fluster. It isn't as though they love fighting all the time, but when they do, they rarely lose, and while you can always make up with each other, you can't unhear some things.

The Judge archetype deals with grief and sadness by surrounding them-selves with pretty things and all forms of art—and a lot of talking with their friends about how they are feeling. Or they may journal about it for hours on end. To everyone outside of their selected trust circle, they will try to pass off that they are fine.

Example of a Perfect Love Connection for the Queen of Swords

- The Queen of Swords—The Judge—Two judges don't make a right? Wrong. These two may talk the house down in a group environment but they just seem to get each other. Usually both partners in a successful pairing of this archetype have careers that satisfy them and keep them challenged enough for a harmonious relationship.

Example of a Troubled Love Connection for the Queen of Swords

- The Knight of Cups—The Romantic—While the romantic may try as hard as they can to paint a pretty picture for this archetype to believe in, they are going to see straight through that and will simply have no time for their games. A short affair, sure, but not a long-term relationship, which suits the Romantic fine in the end anyway.

THE KNIGHT OF SWORDS—THE WARRIOR

When it comes to courting a partner, there is nothing that the Warrior loves more than winning their hand. The harder to get you play, the more attractive you are to this archetype. Allow them to pursue you, not because you should play games with people in order to win their affection, but because this is something they genuinely enjoy. They can, however, be a little relentless, which may overwhelm people who are not used to strong energy. There will be no question that this person is into you, which at least takes the guesswork out of it. They will also not hesitate to make the first move.

The Warrior is the type of lover that sees sex as sacred, and while this is not the only archetype that does so, they may be careful with whom they chose to connect with in this way. They will want to set the mood and take their time. Once they have chosen a partner, they will be willing to try just about anything, as long as it doesn't go against their spiritual code. They love to spice things up or, even better, have their partner plan something special. They may need some coaching, but love a challenge, even in bed, and aim to please.

If they are living in their shadow side, they will be arrogant, dominating, and argumentative. They rarely give a shit what their choices mean for their partner and have a "like it or leave" attitude when it comes to decision making. They can also be selfish and harsh with their words. They will often have a small group of people they have been with on-again, off-again romantically.

Committed relationship? Maybe not for this tarot archetype. They can be very hard to pin down and it's nearly impossible if you are not of the same faith or spiritual path—or at least share a devotion to a similar cause. If you do manage a long-term relationship with a Warrior, expect to spend a lot of time on your own. They are off doing their thing a lot of the time. They will likely have you move around the globe with them too.

Tarot Mucha and Everyday Witch Tarot

In a verbal fight with someone they love, the Warrior will lose their patience very quickly. They will not hesitate to show their dominating side and try to shut down the other person and the conversation with authority. They know where everyone's weaknesses are in their personal armour and will not hesitate to aim for it. If they aren't very verbal, expect them to storm off and go a few rounds with a punching bag to let off steam. They need the space to cool off and think before there can be reconciliation.

When dealing with sadness and grief they will be very quiet. It is very likely that in their mind they are thinking themselves stupid. They will take any loss as though it was personal and could been have avoided if only they were able to conquer what took that person away. Try to get them to talk if you can. They usually feel better once they have let go of all of the thoughts that have been plaguing their mind.

Example of a Perfect Love Connection for the Knight of Swords

- The Queen of Pentacles—The Healer—These two work so well together because their relationship helps give each other purpose. The Healer will be there to patch up the Warrior, either physically or emotionally, and the Warrior will protect all that the Healer cares for, including themselves.

Example of a Troubled Love Connection for the Knight of Swords

- The King of Swords—The Scientist/Specialist—One thinks about things all day and can literally go days without speaking and the other suffers from impulsive speech disorder. The King of Swords is too careful and the Knight of Swords is too rash; they will drive each other crazy.

THE PAGE OF SWORDS–THE DETECTIVE

The Detective will know things about you and your family that you don't even know, because they are very good at observation and also pretty skilled at using the mighty Google. While this is not a very popular courting technique, they just can't help themselves. If they haven't done the background search, they will have likely asked around about the person they are interested in. The detective is usually a great tarot archetype to date. They are quick-witted, inspiring, and really interesting. They listen and remember things, which makes the person they are dating feel special. They will often leave you wanting more too.

As a lover, the Detective can somewhat take sex or leave it. They are more interested in their interpersonal relationships with other people and/

or having good professional and working relationships than being a hot and heavy lover. That is not to say that they won't marry and have children, but their drive may just be low. They will need a lot of coaxing from their partners or they will just simply shut them down when the advance is made.

When living in their shadow aspect the Detective is completely aloof and unable to connect with people. They will live in their own world. They can be hypercritical of their partners and easily suspicious with the people in their lives. They are prone to jealousy and completely unaware of the emotional needs of others.

Steampunk Tarot and Bad Bitches Tarot

In a committed relationship, the Detective will really take the time to get to know and understand their partner. They will want to be in their lives and help them achieve their dreams. They just may not give the most robust emotional support, but they are great listeners and are very honest.

When fighting with a loved one, they will get exasperated and over dramatic. They will take a firm "it's me against them" stance and will expect that if they are fighting with anyone outside the relationship, their partner will automatically take their side. Right or wrong. They can be completely relentless when trying to make their point in an argument and can be un-wavering in their stance unless met with cold, hard facts. Even then, expect some resistance.

This archetype deals with grief and sadness by tearing the situation apart until they can find out what or who is to blame. Everything is someone or something's fault. They can get overwhelmed with loss if there is an injustice attached to it.

Example of a Perfect Love Connection for the Page of Swords

- The King of Swords—The Scientist/Specialist—Both pursue their work with passion and ask multiple questions in search of great an-swers. Neither of them will worry if the other is working late. They just have to make sure they actually see each other once in a while to keep the flame lit.

Example of a Troubled Love Connection for the Page of Swords

- The Queen of Cups—The Mystic—Unfortunately, the Detective will not have any time for the Mystic or what they believe and are able to do. Because this is an intrinsic part of who the Mystic is, this relation-ship won't last beyond a few weeks or months.

EXERCISE: YOUR TAROT COURT LOVE MAP

This personal exploration exercise will allow you to look back on what love tarot archetypes you have been with in your past relationships. It can be useful to see if there have been any partners in your relationships that have played out over and over again. It is also a great way to give real life examples to the tarot court cards in love, which will help you memorise their mean-ings, actions, and behaviours when they come up in a tarot reading.

This exercise is just another layer of information you can use when it comes to building your catalogue of information about the tarot court.

The worksheet is designed to look like a map, which is a visual rep-resentation of your journey in love.

Questions for the Road Map
and Further Exploration

Who was your first love?

Who do you identify with the most now?

When you are in your shadow side, what love archetype do you most embody?

What lessons do you believe your love archetype can teach you?

If you are in a relationship, what love archetype is your partner or significant other?

Do you feel you have learned anything new about them?

If you are single, what love archetype is someone you would love to be with? Why?

What love archetype is someone you would not like to be with? Why?

EXERCISE: SEEKING A NEW LOVER TAROT SPREAD

This tarot spread uses the information about the tarot court to help you find out a little or a lot about the next person who is going to come into your life or your querent's life. For those tarot readers who do not usually use the tarot for predictive work, this can be a fun reflective exercise or it can be a great way to dip your toes into the predictive pool.

You can use the information in this book to flesh out the personality, how they are in love, and what to be on the lookout for when you meet new people.

1. Take your chosen tarot deck out and separate the tarot court cards from the pack. Place the rest of the deck aside for now.

2. Hold the tarot court cards in your hands and close your eyes Think about bringing love to your life and, if you are adept at creative visualisation, carry out one about your ideal future relationship. It is highly recommended not to think of any one person in particular as that will interfere with the reading. You want to leave this open by not targeting people you may already be interested in. They may pop up anyway.

3. Shuffle the tarot court cards while still holding as much of the energy you focused on. When you feel ready, fan the cards out in front of you and pick two cards that you feel most drawn to. Place the them in the spread positions A and B as shown below.

4. Now place the remaining court cards back in the deck and shuffle the cards until you feel ready. Then fan or cut the deck and select the remaining cards. Place them in positions 1, 2, and 3 as shown in the following tarot card layout.

Position A. This is your future partner's outward personality, the one they show the public and workplace. The one most people will know them by and how you may see them when you first meet.

Position B. This is your future partner's deeper personality. You can learn about how they express and deal with sadness and shadow things that they struggle with. It is the part of their soul that also has great gifts.

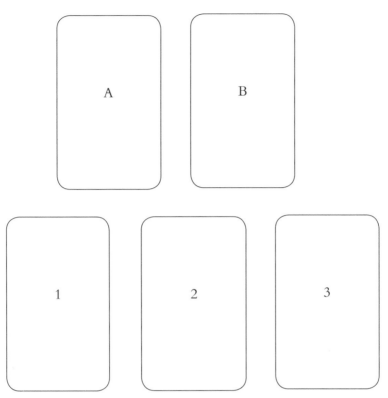

Position 1. This is their work. It can be very literal or take some digging. The suits will give you some big clues and so will the position of the card in the suit.

Position 2. This will give you clues as to how you are going to meet.

Position 3. This is the major lesson and theme of the relationship with this person.

EXERCISE: HEALING RELATIONSHIPS TAROT SPREAD

This tarot spread and exercise has been developed to help you heal and move on from past relationships. This can be done completely solo, but if you ever get the chance to do this with an ex, I can personally recommend it as a deeply revealing and healing experience. I recommend that you do not carry out this exercise with an ex when you are feeling extremely emotional, as it may be too much and the reading may end up muddy. Some exes should be avoided like the plague. You broke up for a reason, after all.

This is also not designed to be a way to spy on your ex to see what they are up to. It is a healing exercise that can bring closure and a chance to leave negative traits in the past without carrying them into your next relationship.

Before you begin this exercise, choose how you want to read the cards. Do you want to select the cards diviner style where you shuffle the cards, cut the deck, and reveal them without ever seeing their fronts or do you want to work intuitive picture style? Intuitive picture style reading is where you go through the deck with the images face up and select the cards based on the images and your intuition of what you feel represents the layout's position best.

You will need two complete tarot decks for this exercise.

1. Take the first chosen tarot deck out and separate the tarot court cards from the pack. Set the rest of the deck aside for now.

2. Shuffle the court cards and pull a card or intuitively select the tarot court card that is the significator for you in that relationship and place it in position significator A.

3. Repeat the first two steps with the second chosen tarot deck and place the card in position significator B, or have the person you are reading with (e.g. your ex) carry out the first two steps with their deck.

4. Replace the court cards back into their respective decks.

5. Take the first deck and shuffle the cards again to get the court cards back in the mix. Focus on your part of the relationship, your experiences, your energy, and the half that you brought to the whole. When you are ready, cut the deck and place the rest of the cards in the numerical order as shown in the following layout or intuitively select the cards and place them in positions 1 to 5.

6. Take the second deck and reshuffle the cards. Now bring your attention to your ex's energy and role in the relationship. When you are ready, cut the deck and place the rest of the cards in the numerical order as shown in the layout or intuitively select the cards and place them in positions 6 to 10. If you are reading with another person (e.g., your ex), have them carry out these steps with their deck.

Querant

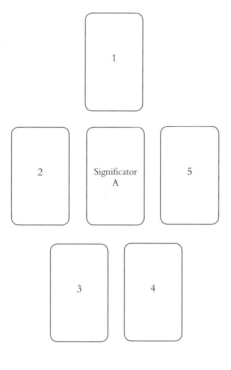

Ex

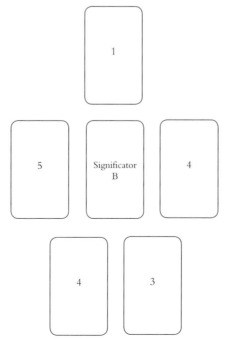

Position Meanings

1 and 6—The Mask—The surface issue that is leaving the relationship unhealed

2 and 7—The Past—The past event or belief that is still affecting the relationship

3 and 8—The Release—What needs to be forgiven and released in order for the relationship to move forward (even if you are never again to be romantically involved with each other)

4 and 9—The Wound—What you want the other party to acknowledge, hear, or understand

5 and 10—The Step—The next step forward towards healing for you both

~ Ten ~
TAROT COURT POP CULTURE REPRESENTATIONS

There are millions of fantastic characters that live in our hearts and minds. They come to us in movies, comics, television, video games, and books, and can shape the way that we see the world. The connection between tarot and the world of popular culture has been edging closer together each year. We have fan-created decks for everything and even now have fully endorsed tarot decks for popular television shows.

Below is a series of characters and their tarot court archetype assignment. You may see these differently and that is okay. It is just another layer to add to the way we view the cards. If we are able to see the cards as a popular character, we can get to know them in a deeper way. It is also a wonderful way to learn the cards for people who often struggle to remember card meanings.

While I maintain that the tarot court archetypes are gender neutral, it is not very well represented in popular culture. I have endeavoured to provide more than one example of each for some balance. Essentially, characters are usually more aligned to being good or evil, which is actually great for understanding manifestations of both the shadow and light aspects of the tarot court.

There is usually an abundance of similar archetypes in stories as well, which is why not every character in their worlds has been explored. I hope that this is the beginning of a long list of tarot pop culture archetypes for your tarot practice.

Characters would also be boring if they didn't evolve and grow. That is one of the reasons we bond and continue to invest our time into them, their worlds, and their adventures. So while they may change into different court card archetypes as their stories grow, these are some of the examples that still hold true or that have been impactful.

King of Swords—The Scientist/Specialist

Tyrion Lannister—(*Game of Thrones*)—Tyrion is the smartest man in the room, and he is not a humble man when it comes to his intelligence—because it is his armour. While his intellect would have been his natural inclination, he has made it his life's work to arm himself with knowledge. He is excellent counsel for those who lead and a master strategist. Lord Varys is another brilliant embodiment in the *Game of Thrones* world of the King of Swords.

Spock—(*Star Trek*)—The King of Swords has always been my Spock card. Brilliant, focused, a leader, and someone who is dedicated to their work. As a half-Vulcan, a species of aliens in the Star Trek universe that hold logic and reason well above emotion, he carries this filter across everything that he does and says.

Other Scientists—Sheldon Cooper (*The Big Bang Theory*), Bruce Banner/ Hulk (Marvel Comics), Dr. Emmett Brown (*Back to the Future*)

Your personal picks for the Scientist in pop culture:

_____

_____

_____

QUEEN OF SWORDS–THE JUDGE

Cersei Lannister—(*Game of Thrones*)—Get in this woman's way and judge you she will. She will also be your executioner, although she won't be the one doing the dirty work. Cersei is a wonderful example of the shadow Queen of Swords. Clever, cruel, cunning, and not backing down to anyone. She knows when to speak, when to be silent, and what words are going to get her what she ultimately wants.

Miranda Hobbs—(*Sex and the City*)—This high-powered lawyer has often been seen by the SATC fandom as the most judgemental of the four friends that the show centres around. She struggles the most with putting anything but her career first and often sees things from a more intellectual point of view. She is also extremely loyal and caring and never hesitates to help her friends with her legal smarts or her friendly ear.

Your personal picks for the Judge in pop culture:

_____

_____

_____

KNIGHT OF SWORDS–THE WARRIOR

Wonder Woman—(D.C. Comics)—Represented in the 2017 movie, Wonder Woman is a near perfect example of the Warrior. She is not at all harsh even though she has been trained from a young age and surrounded by other warriors her whole life. She acts and speaks her mind (even though it was not something many women did in at the time of World War I) and she knows that the reason for her existence is to be the one who protects others. She is a wonderful embodiment of a warrior who has their head and heart working together.

Lee Ju-fan/Bruce Lee—(*Enter the Dragon* and *Bruce Lee: A Warrior's Journey*)—While you could put any of Bruce Lee's performances here as a wonderful representation of the Warrior, he was an exceptional warrior himself.

There has only ever been one Bruce Lee, and watching his films, biopics, and documentaries or reading about his life will show you a lot about this archetype.

Other Warriors—The Bride (*Kill Bill: Vol. 1 & 2*), Rocky Balboa (*Rocky*)

Your personal picks for the Warrior in pop culture:

_____

_____

_____

PAGE OF SWORDS—THE DETECTIVE

Sherlock Holmes—(*Sherlock Holmes* by Arthur Conan Doyle)—While this Detective is not acting inside a job in law enforcement, he is a wonderful character for the Detective archetype. He works with Scotland Yard in many of his incarnations, often being one or three steps ahead of them and able to do the things they cannot. He cuts through the crap and gives straightforward deductions and solutions. Because of his quirks and often inability to read social cues, he is definitely in the Page element. He is one of the most well known Detective characters in history.

Nancy Drew—(*Nancy Drew Mystery Series* by Carolyn Keene)—This teenage Detective is as iconic as Sherlock—wise and daring beyond her years and an inspiration for may modern incarnations of this archetype. Independent, brilliant at persuading people, and self-sufficient, her character has endured, evolved, and impacted millions of people.

Other Detectives—Luther, Miss Phryne Fisher, Veronica Mars

Your personal picks for the Detective in pop culture:

_____

_____

_____

KING OF PENTACLES–THE MANAGER

Jules Ostin—(*The Intern*)—While the movie is a little bit of a millennial dream, Jules finds not only her business growing but also her responsibility to the people around her. Jules not only has to face the challenges that running her wildly successful company gives her but also has to learn how to juggle her family life as well. Flaws and challenges and all, she remains a great manager to her employees and stays true to her vision for the company.

Scrooge McDuck—(Carl Barks) & Ebenezer Scrooge—(*A Christmas Carol* by Charles Dickens)—The reason they are put here together is that Scrooge McDuck was inspired by Ebenezer and actually holds a lot of the more positive sides to this character. His character did start out as more of a miser, but this was not the case for the entire run of Scrooge. He was the beloved Uncle Scrooge to Huey, Duey, and Louie and was generous with his mountains of gold. Ebenezer on the other hand, needed quite the kick before he saw the light. A strict and stingy business owner and a loner, he is a reminder of what happens when our greed out grows our heart.

Other Managers—Ron Swanson (*Parks and Recreation*), Dwight Schrute and Michael Scott (*The Office*)

Your personal picks for the Manager in pop culture:

_____

_____

_____

QUEEN OF PENTACLES–THE HEALER

Dr. Michaela Quinn—(*Dr. Quinn, Medicine Woman*)—Braving a new frontier is one thing, raising three children who you adopted and convincing a whole town you shouldn't be burnt at the stake is a quite another. This show ran for six seasons and had two movies in the franchise. Dr. Quinn is a beloved and pioneering healer.

Captain Benjamin Franklin 'Hawkeye' Pierce—(*M*A*S*H*)—Hawkeye is one of TV's most memorable doctors, and the show ran for over 250 episodes. Extreme situations paired with the constant fight for survival—of not only their patients but of the members of the 4077th M*A*S*H—makes for an enduring archetype.

Other Healers—Dr. McCoy (*Star Trek*), Dr. Greg House (*House M.D.*) Dr. Chandler (*St. Elsewhere*), Nurse Carla Espinosa (*Scrubs*)

Your personal picks for the Healer in pop culture:

_____

_____

_____

Knight of Pentacles—The Soldier

Captain John H. Miller—(*Saving Private Ryan*)—Going through more physically, mentally, and emotionally difficult experiences than most, simply because it is his duty to do so, Captain Miller had a lot of responsibility on his shoulders and took his role extremely seriously. He also made the largest sacrifice you can in the name of duty.

Forrest Gump—(*Forrest Gump*)—This is one loving and extremely loyal character. He is loyal to the people he loves and to his country. When he sets his mind to do something, he just does it, no matter the challenge to his mind, body, and soul.

Other soldiers—Maverick (*Top Gun*), Staff Sergeant William James (*The Hurt Locker*)

Your personal picks for the Soldier in pop culture:

_____

_____

_____

Page of Pentacles—The Naturalist

Hagrid—(the Harry Potter series)—Hagrid's love for animals is as big as he is. Hagrid is trustworthy, kind, and golden-hearted. He is also very childlike when it comes to his naivety around what is considered a safe animal to have around children. He became the Keeper of the Keys and Grounds at Hogwarts after he was expelled because he wouldn't hand over a beloved pet (which was a giant freaking spider).

The Hobbits—(the Lord of the Ring series)—The hobbits are practical and simple and rarely do anything that others would see as adventurous. They tend nature's garden, they love flora and fauna and anything that grows. They work and live off the land and have been seen by many as living a simple life. While the central hobbits do go on great adventures, they still maintain their down-to-earth hearts.

Other examples of the Naturalist—Dr. Doolittle, the Lorax

Your personal picks for the Naturalist in pop culture:

_____

_____

_____

King of Wands—The Entrepreneur

Oprah Winfrey—If there were a movie made by Oprah Winfrey, she would be on the top of my list. She is a cultural icon, so I am including her here. A media magnate and household name, she embodies the Entrepreneur.

Daenerys Targaryen—(*Game of Thrones*)—Daenerys started from nothing to become one heck of a leader, and maybe by the time this book is published, the ruler of what is left of the seven kingdoms after the winter is over. She is my pick for the Entrepreneur as she has not only been able to amass an incredible number of supporters, but she has often gone it alone, done what no one else had thought even possible, and is the ruler of her own domain. Plus she has dragons.

Steve Jobs—(*Jobs*)—Like Apple or not, Steve jobs changed the landscape by turning technology into a lifestyle. The path to success is shown as rocky and he does some questionable things along the way. However, he created a brand that is a monolith.

Other Entrepreneurs in pop culture—Joy (*Joy* (film)), Samantha Jones (*Sex and the City*) Mark Zuckerberg (*The Social Network*)

Your personal picks for the Entrepreneur in pop culture:

_____

_____

_____

QUEEN OF WANDS—THE PERFORMER

Carrie Bradshaw—(*Sex and the City*)—Carrie is a writer and someone who documents human behaviours in relationships and sex. You can also say that her wardrobe is just as much a part of her persona as her work or personality. Carrie also tends to lose herself momentarily in her relationships, which many Performers do. They crave the experience that people can give them and want to enter their world, ultimately using that experience as fuel for their art.

Rachel Marron—(*The Bodyguard*)—Even from a young age, Rachel overshadowed her sister to become the star. She is an entertainer in every sense of the word, with a number of talents. She is a commanding and magnetic personality with a lot of sass and a control freak to boot. Her whole life is like a performance and her close interpersonal relationships suffer for it.

Other Performers—The *Dreamgirls* cast, Ray Charles (*Ray*) Satine (*Moulin Rouge*)

Your personal picks for the Performer in pop culture:

_____

_____

_____

KNIGHT OF WANDS—THE ADVENTURER

Lara Croft—(*Tomb Raider*)—Whether she is in video game format or being played by an actress on the big screen, this British Adventurer is always on a quest to find what has been lost and understand what has alluded people for thousands of years. She is seen moving around the globe regularly and speaks multiple languages, ancient and modern.

Indiana Jones—(*Indiana Jones*)—One of the most iconic Adventurers of our time. Indiana was born into a family of archaeologists and keeps the family legacy alive in his chosen profession. He has helped save the world a number of times and travelled to all parts of our lovely planet. He is quick on his feet and able to hold his own in dangerous situations.

Other adventurers—Nathan Drake (*Uncharted*), The Doctor (*Doctor Who*)

Your personal picks for the Adventurer in pop culture:

_____

_____

_____

THE PAGE OF WANDS—PETER PAN

Peter Pan—(Disney's *Peter Pan*)—Well we can't have this archetype represented without the namesake. Whether you see Peter Pan as a spirit that keeps souls young, steals children in the night, or is himself a lost boy, he is the very representation of a character that never wants to grow up.

Shaggy—(*Scooby-Doo*)—For the younger generation watching the cartoons, many of the stoner jokes will thankfully go over their head, but Shaggy has a dog for a best friend and always seems to be the last one to understand what is going on. He's certainly not looking to grow up and change his care-free, food-filled lifestyle anytime soon.

Other Peter Pans—Tripp (*Failure to Launch*), Kevin Pearson (*This Is Us*), Jack McFarland (*Will & Grace*)

Your personal picks for Peter Pan in pop culture:

_____

_____

_____

THE KING OF CUPS–HADES

Professor Snape—(the Harry Potter series)—Readers and audiences were never really sure of this character's true motives and allegiances until the very end. He walked the line of darkness and had little patience for anything that he deemed to be immature or lacking in character. A deep character indeed with wonderful layers.

Aragorn—(the Lord of the Rings series)—Nothing short of the end of the world gets this reluctant king out of hiding. He seems to see right through peoples' façades and is one of the very few humans who is able to be in the elves' presence without them recoiling. He is deep, loyal, and not afraid at the end to face the darkness within himself or in his enemies for the greater good of his people.

Other Hades—Hades (Disney's *Hercules*), Batman (DC Comics)

Your personal picks for Hades in pop culture:

_____

_____

_____

THE QUEEN OF CUPS—THE MYSTIC

The Oracle—(*The Matrix*)—Her name really does say it all. Not only is she revered for her abilities, but she is also the perfect Mystic, asking the hero questions to help him acquire his own answers.

Jillian and Sally Owens—(*Practical Magic*)—Magic is in these sisters' blood. Their whole family has been persecuted by the townsfolk for their history and gifts, but in the end, these sisters are able to bring people together and closer to their own magic. They can hear each other when they cry out for help, know it's the other on the phone before picking it up, and can cast miraculous spells. They also kind of fly.

Other Mystics—River Tam (*Firefly*), Carrie White (*Carrie*), Oda Mae Brown (*Ghost*), Madame Serena (*Teen Witch*), Dr. Strange (Marvel Comics)

Your personal picks for the Mystic in pop culture:

_____

_____

_____

THE KNIGHT OF CUPS—THE ROMANTIC

Casanova—(*Casanova* (film))—Set in a romantic city during a highly romanticised time, this young Romantic took pride in bedding as many women as he could. It didn't matter if they were religious, married, or betrothed—they were all fair game. A well-earned reputation that is passed on in the end to the next Casanova.

Romeo and Juliet—(*Romeo and Juliet*)—What is more romantic than dying for love, right? Not to mention breaking their parents' hearts and going behind their backs. They are the definition of intoxicating and all-consuming love.

Other romantics—James Bond (the James Bond series), Alfie (*Alfie* (film))

Your personal picks for the Romantic in pop culture:

_____

_____

_____

THE PAGE OF CUPS—THE EMPATH

Deanna Troi—(*Star Trek: The Next Generation*)—a ship's counsellor who rose in rank to become a commander in Starfleet. She was an important part of many negotiations in space. Deanna had powerful empathic abilities, which were part of her genes. She is able to tell if people are lying and tune people out who might harm her (depending on the alien race). Deanna was a well-educated woman who also studied psychology.

Phoebe Halliwell—(*Charmed*)—While this is a gift and power that this charmed sister grows into in later seasons, her first experience with her powers shows her and the audience what it can feel like to be an Empath in the extreme. Not only is empathy a power she has, but working as an advice columnist, she uses her big heart in her career too. Phoebe also held a BA in psychology, which is another aligned field to the Empath.

Your personal picks for the Empath in pop culture:

_____

_____

_____

EXERCISE: POP CULTURE TAROT BINGO

This is a fun game that you can play the next time you are watching your favourite TV show or a movie, or even when you are reading a book. You can photocopy the following cards or just copy them by hand. There are four bingo grids so you can even invite your tarot friends over for a viewing party of your favourite show or new movie and play the game together. Each player or team (if there is more than four of you) gets a different bingo board.

This game is also a way to see how characters grow and move into different roles throughout their story arcs. It can reflect the ways we do this ourselves. When you have filled in a row, you can rejoice by exclaiming "Bingo!" Prizes include understanding the tarot better and being awesome.

You will need:

- The bingo playing boards
- Pen or markers
- Your selected media (a television show or movie)

HOW TO PLAY TAROT COURT CARD BINGO

While watching your chosen media, look out for characters that represent the tarot archetypes on your bingo sheet. When characters show a classic characteristic or behaviour, colour in the box and write down the character's name. Continue until someone fills in a line horizontally, vertically, or diagonally and enthusiastically yells, "BINGO!"

BINGO CARD 1

King of Cups—Hades Moody, broody character, just stares instead of speaking As represented by:	King of Wands—Entrepreneur Character starts a company or side hustle business As represented by:	Page of Pentacles—Naturalist Character seeks out comfort from an animal As represented by:	Page of Cups—Empath Character picks up on unspoken emotions of another character As represented by:
Knight of Swords—Warrior Starts a fight As represented by:	Knight of Cups—Romantic Character declares their love for another character As represented by:	Queen of Wands—Performer Character takes to the stage As represented by:	Page of Swords—Detective Solves a problem, finds a clue As represented by:
King of Pentacles—Manager Character worries about money or finances As represented by:	Queen of Pentacles—Healer Character tends to a wound or nurses someone As represented by:	Knight of Wands—Adventurer Gets on a plane or boat for a trip As represented by:	Queen of Swords—Judge Mediates an argument or misunderstanding As represented by:
Queen of Cups—Mystic Character knows what is going to happen before it does As represented by:	Knight of Pentacles—Soldier Character acts out of loyalty As represented by:	King of Swords—Scientist Character proves another wrong As represented by:	Page of Wands—Peter Pan Character runs away from a problem As represented by:

BINGO CARD 2

Knight of Wands—Adventurer Gets on a plane or boat for a trip As represented by:	Page of Swords—Detective Solves a problem, finds a clue As represented by:	Page of Pentacles—Naturalist Character seeks out comfort from an animal As represented by:	Knight of Swords—Warrior Starts a fight As represented by:
Page of Cups—Empath Character picks up on unspoken emotions of another character As represented by:	Knight of Cups—Romantic Character declares their love for another character As represented by:	King of Wands—Entrepreneur Character starts a company or side hustle business As represented by:	Queen of Pentacles—Healer Character tends to a wound or nurses someone As represented by:
King of Pentacles—Manager Character worries about money or finances As represented by:	Queen of Wands—Performer Character takes to the stage As represented by:	King of Cups—Hades Moody, broody character, just stares instead of speaking As represented by:	Queen of Swords—Judge Mediates an argument or misunderstanding As represented by:
Page of Wands—Peter Pan Character runs away from a problem As represented by:	Queen of Cups—Mystic Character knows what is going to happen before it does As represented by:	Knight of Pentacles—Soldier Character acts out of loyalty As represented by:	King of Swords—Scientist Character proves another wrong As represented by:

Bingo Card 3

King of Wands— Entrepreneur Character starts a company or side hustle business As represented by:	Queen of Pentacles— Healer Character tends to a wound or nurses someone As represented by:	Knight of Cups— Romantic Character declares their love for another character As represented by:	Page of Cups— Empath Character picks up on unspoken emotions of another character As represented by:
Knight of Wands— Adventurer Gets on a plane or boat for a trip As represented by:	Knight of Swords—Warrior Starts a fight As represented by:	Queen of Wands— Performer Character takes to the stage As represented by:	Page of Swords— Detective Solves a problem, finds a clue As represented by:
King of Pentacles— Manager Character worries about money or finances As represented by:	Page of Pentacles— Naturalist Character seeks out comfort from an animal As represented by:	King of Cups— Hades Moody, broody character, just stares instead of speaking As represented by:	Queen of Swords—Judge Mediates an argument or misunderstanding As represented by:
King of Swords— Scientist Character proves another wrong As represented by:	Page of Wands— Peter Pan Character runs away from a problem As represented by:	Queen of Cups— Mystic Character knows what is going to happen before it does As represented by:	Knight of Pentacles—Soldier Character acts out of loyalty As represented by:

BINGO CARD 4

Page of Cups—Empath Character picks up on unspoken emotions of another character As represented by:	King of Pentacles—Manager Character worries about money or finances As represented by:	Page of Pentacles—Naturalist Character seeks out comfort from an animal As represented by:	King of Wands—Entrepreneur Character starts a company or side hustle business As represented by:
King of Cups—Hades Moody, broody character, just stares instead of speaking As represented by:	Knight of Cups—Romantic Character declares their love for another character As represented by:	Queen of Wands—Performer Character takes to the stage As represented by:	Page of Swords—Detective Solves a problem, finds a clue As represented by:
Queen of Swords—Judge Mediates an argument or misunderstanding As represented by:	Queen of Pentacles—Healer Character tends to a wound or nurses someone As represented by:	Knight of Wands—Adventurer Gets on a plane or boat for a trip As represented by:	Knight of Swords—Warrior Starts a fight As represented by:
Knight of Pentacles—Soldier Character acts out of loyalty As represented by:	King of Swords—Scientist Character proves another wrong As represented by:	Page of Wands—Peter Pan Character runs away from a problem As represented by:	Queen of Cups—Mystic Character knows what is going to happen before it does As represented by:

EXERCISE: REFLECTION QUESTIONS ON TAROT AND POP CULTURE

In modern society, we consume a lot of media. Whether we make the connection to the tarot or not, we are being shown representations of the tarot archetypes every time we watch our favourite show or go to the movies. You can use these reflective questions about pop culture and the tarot for your developing knowledge of these concepts.

- Is there a recurring tarot court card archetype in most TV shows, movies, and books?
- Why do you think that is?
- Do you feel that reflects real life or do we like to live out other existences through unfamiliar archetypes?
- What are some of the rarer tarot court card archetypes in pop culture?
- If you were a character in a TV show, who would you be and what tarot court card archetype is that?

EXERCISE: CREATIVE PROBLEM-SOLVING WITH THE COURT ARCHETYPES

This exercise is a great way to see how the different archetypes of the tarot court would act and consider an obstacle. It is a way for you to see your possibilities through different lenses.

For this exercise, you will need a tarot deck, a notebook, and a pen.

Step 1. Separate out your court cards from the rest of the deck and set them aside the other cards.

Step 2. Write down your problem, challenge, or obstacle.

Step 3. Shuffle your deck of cards that has the major arcana and the minor arcana while holding the problem, challenge, or obstacle in your mind. It is best to focus on one at a time, because you can carry out this exercise with as many challenges as you wish.

Step 4. Cut the deck as you desire and lay out the following cards.

Card 1—Where you are at with the challenge

Card 2—What you may not know that is affecting you or it

Step 4. Reflect on those two cards for a moment and take into consideration any insight gleaned from them.

Step 5. Take the pile of court cards and shuffle them while focusing on the challenge.

Step 6. When ready, fan the cards out, select four court cards and place them beneath your first two cards.

Step 7. With your knowledge of these archetypes, ask:

- How would each of these tarot court archetypes tackle the challenge?
- What would be their next move?
- What would these archetypes consider as a helpful resource or ally?
- What weakness does their approach show?
- Which one of these is your most likely next move based on past experience?
- Which one of these is the most surprising next move?

For Advanced Readers

Step 8. Gather your pile of cards with the major arcana and the minor arcana and shuffle the deck again. Cut the deck and place a card under each of the court cards to see what the likely outcome of these actions will be for the challenge. If this is likely to confuse you, please do not feel as if you need to carry this part out. This is predominantly a problem-solving exercise.

You now have four sets of experts looking at your challenge or obstacle from differing perspectives, offering you different paths forward and their most likely outcome. When I use the tarot for problem-solving, I usually have an "Aha!" moment, even if the supporting card is not as favourable as it could be. Always trust your intuition.

∿ Eleven ⌒
THE COURT CARDS
TAROT SPREADS

Each court card in the tarot has a specific gift. The specially created tarot spreads can be used to explore how the court card can aid your spiritual journey and deepen your understanding of the tarot. They can also give you clues as to how to use them when they appear in a tarot reading.

If a court card or two shows up in your reading and you get stuck, come back and look at the gift each card has been assigned in this section. See if that helps you understand the card and its meaning in the position better.

I always recommend that you journal your tarot readings, including the date you conducted the reading and the tarot deck that you used. There are prompting questions included that are outside of the tarot spread itself. These are very powerful questions that you can use to connect to the tarot court card, and I recommend including your discoveries along with your tarot reading in your tarot journal.

The following tarot spreads are all nine card tarot spreads so it is recommended that you allow for the time to read a larger tarot spread before you begin.

Instructions:

To start these tarot readings, go through the tarot deck that you are using and take the relevant court card out of the deck (for example, the Page of Cups, Knight of Pentacles, etc.). Place this card in the position of 1. Then shuffle the rest of the deck while concentrating on this card. Imagine that it is standing right in front of you. (You can close your eyes while you are shuffling if that helps.) What is its aura like? How does it feel? How do you feel around it?

When you feel ready, stop shuffling and cut the deck in your regular fashion. Then place the cards as indicated in each exercise below. The following layout is for all of the tarot court gift spreads.

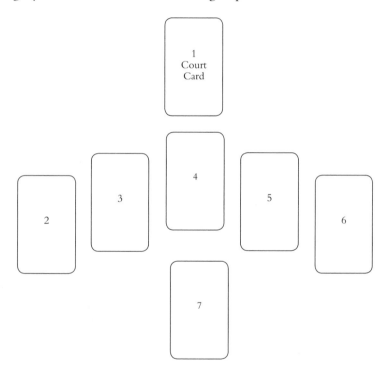

THE PAGE OF CUPS—GIFT—EMOTION

Elemental Associations

Page—Earth

Cups—Water

Like all pages, the Page of Cups is full of potential and has the purest energy of their court card family. Because of this, the Page of Cups can help you connect with your emotions and show what an amazing gift being in touch with your emotional body can be. Emotions can rule us. They can make or break our day when they are extreme or if we lack the other elements like intelligent (air) or grounding (earth) by helping balance it out. For this tarot spread exercise, however, you are going to be creating a safe space to really delve into your deep emotional well and reflect on its impact and power in your life.

Take some time to connect with your emotions while you are shuffling the deck. Remember the last time you felt full of positive emotions. What was going on in your life when that happened? Then, think about a time where you were faced with more difficult emotions like loss and sadness, for these also have gifts and lessons for you.

EXERCISE

Place the cards as follows:

1. The Page of Cups—the significator card

2. How can I express my emotional self better?

3. What can I let go of to help unblock any negative emotions?

4. What can I do more of to connect to my emotional self?

5. What do I need to let go of emotionally?

6. How can I connect to the Page of Cups better as a tarot card?

7. What lesson can the Page of Cups share with my clients?

THE KNIGHT OF CUPS—GIFT—ROMANCE

Elemental Associations

Knight—Fire

Cups—Water

The Knight of Cups believes in love, love, love. They are all about love. They write songs and poetry about love. They battle for love and they are in love with being in love. Being the Knight of Romance, they are often triggered by love and romance. They can also tend to see everything through rose-coloured glasses. We all need balance, and romance is only one part of a relationship. This tarot spread is a chance for you to explore romance and how it can bring some spice into your life and help you fall in love with your life.

Take some time to connect to your romantic side. When was the last time you were shown romance? Or what would a romantic date be like for you? What comes to the forefront of your mind when you think about romance?

EXERCISE

Place the cards as follows:

1. The Knight of Cups—the significator card

2. How can I connect with my inner Knight of Romance, my romantic side?

3. How can I bring more pleasure into my life?

4. What is my love code; how do I like to express my love?

5. What potential romantic baggage can I let go of?

6. How can I connect to the Knight of Cups better as a tarot card?

7. What lesson can the Knight of Cups share with my clients?

THE QUEEN OF CUPS–GIFT–INTUITION

Elemental Associations

Queen—Water

Cups—Water

The Queen of Cups holds the gift of inner knowing within her. This is intensified as she is double water (queens and cups are both water). This is a gift that flows through all of us, and by calling us to embrace the inner Mystic within, we are able to walk our paths in alignment with our highest good. She knows that when intuition is embraced, developed, and acted upon, it becomes a strong ally in our lives.

Take some time to connect with the Mystic within you. When was the last time you received an intuitive hit? Do you have any active "clairs" such as clairvoyance and clairsentience? Where in your body does your inner knowing sit?

EXERCISE

Place the cards as follows:

1. The Queen of Cups—the significator card

2. What messages do my guides want me to know about my intuitive gifts?

3. What do I need in order to develop my intuition further?

4. How can I release any fears around acting on my intuition?

5. What kind of mystic could I be?

6. How can I connect to the Queen of Cups better as a tarot card?

7. What lesson can the Queen of Cups share with my clients?

THE KING OF CUPS—GIFT—SEXUALITY

Elemental Associations

King—Air

Cups—Water

Sexuality is personal. It is my belief that it is not something that can be labelled and put in a box. The King of Cups knows who he is and knows that sex is a powerful force. He understands the creation, the destruction, the allure, the seduction, and the darkness that can be around sexuality. As a society, we have cheapened sex. We sell everything from hamburgers to cars with sex. We encourage children to grow up too soon and reward those who use their sexuality to gain fame and power more than talent in some areas. Or we repress it completely because we fear its power. The King of Cups is above that. He wants you to explore the real divine power of your sexuality, however that looks and feels to you and your life.

Now take some time to connect with your sacral chakra and your sexual power. What do you find sexually attractive? Does sex make you feel uncomfortable? Are you comfortable expressing what you want and need sexually? Do you feel connected to your sexuality—why or why not?

EXERCISE

Place the cards as follows:

1. The King of Cups—the significator card

2. How can I connect more with my inner Eros (god of sex and pleasure)?

3. What area of my sexuality could I express more?

4. How does my sexuality connect with my spirituality?

5. What does the King of Cups have to teach me about sexuality?

6. How can I connect to the King of Cups better as a tarot card?

7. What lesson can the King of Cups share with my clients?

THE PAGE OF PENTACLES–GIFT–NATURE

Elemental Associations

Page—Earth

Pentacles—Earth

This page is the closest to nature out of all of the court cards in the tarot. The Page of Pentacles reminds us that there is nothing more nurturing to the soul, no greater connection to be had to that of the natural world. They know that Mother Nature can teach us everything if we only take the time to explore and the patience to allow it to unfold in front of us. Nature takes her time and so too does the Page of Pentacles.

Take some time to connect with nature (even if you are inside—but extra gold star points if you are doing this reading and exercise outside). What is your favourite place in nature? Why do you feel and think you are drawn to those places? How do you feel when something takes time to develop or complete? What is your power animal/spirit animal and why do you think that is?

EXERCISE

Place the cards as follows:

1. The Page of Pentacles—the significator card

2. What are my natural gifts?

3. How can I aid my journey to completeness?

4. How can I bring forward my potential?

5. What does the Page of Pentacles have to teach me about growth?

6. How can I connect to the Page of Pentacles better as a tarot card?

7. What lesson can the Page of Pentacles share with my clients?

THE KNIGHT OF PENTACLES–GIFT–ENDURANCE

Elemental Associations

Knight—Fire

Pentacles—Earth

This is the Knight that you want to have on your side for the long journey of life. The Knight of Pentacles has reserves of energy, conviction, and faith that others can only dream of. They are just as passionate about their quests and causes, but they ensure that they are doing everything that they can to go the distance. This knight has the gift of endurance and can teach us much about diligence and longevity. Like all knights, he is called to action, so don't think this is just a passive energy. It is the one that all champions know can mean the difference between defeat and victory.

Take some time to connect with your fortitude and endurance. When was the last time something tested your endurance? What do you do in your life to prepare for the long term or long term journey, goals, or projects? Do you keep the long term in mind when you act? What comes up for you when you think of slowing down?

EXERCISE

Place the cards as follows:

1. The Knight of Pentacles—the significator card

2. What are my strengths?

3. What have I been resisting?

4. How can I aid my long term spiritual journey?

5. What does the Knight of Pentacles have to teach me about steadiness?

6. How can I connect to the Knight of Pentacles better as a tarot card?

7. What lesson can the Knight of Pentacles share with my clients?

THE QUEEN OF PENTACLES–GIFT–HEALING

Elemental Associations

Queen—Water

Pentacles—Earth

The Queen of Pentacles holds the sacred gift of healing within her. She understands that we need to allow all things to flow, just as holding on to anything too long creates disease. She knows the healing power of laughter, love, sweat, and tears. She knows the healing gifts that are found in nature all around us. She brings the elements of water and earth together for powerful healing magic. This is her gift and she wants all of us to help heal each other and ourselves. When we heal ourselves, we are a much more powerful force in the world and can fully share our gifts with others.

Take some time to connect with the healer within you. What heals you? Is there a special place in nature that you like to go to when you need to recharge? What does health feel like to you?

EXERCISE

Place the cards as follows:

1. The Queen of Pentacles—the significator card

2. What area in my life could use some restoration?

3. What do I need in order to find balance in my life?

4. Where can I release and relieve my diseases in my body and energy fields?

5. What kind of healer can I be?

6. How can I connect to the Queen of Pentacles better as a tarot card?

7. What lesson can the Queen of Pentacles share with my clients?

THE KING OF PENTACLES–GIFT–STABILITY

Elemental Associations

King—Air

Pentacles—Earth

The King of Pentacles sits steady and firm on his throne, and there is good reason for this. The decisions that he has made in life have been carefully considered and planned to ensure that he is secure in his position and within himself. It take a lot to shake the King of Pentacles because his foundations are strong. This gift can be lent to all areas of your life: work, career, spirituality, relationships, and health. The King of Pentacles can show you how to master consistency, balance, and cohesion. The King of Pentacles knows that the mundane matters, that it is all connected and builds a flourishing reality if only we pay attention and do the work that it requires.

Take some time to connect with your foundations. Do your foundations in each area of your life feel strong and well tended? What areas require more consistency? What daily actions can you take to bring more balance and cohesion into your life? What does stability look and feel like to you?

Place the cards as follows:

1. The King of Pentacles—the significator card

2. How can I bring more physical stability into my life?

3. How can I bring more emotional stability into my life?

4. How can I bring more spiritual stability into my life?

5. What does the King of Pentacles have to teach me about personal boundaries?

6. How can I connect to the King of Pentacles better as a tarot card?

7. What lesson can the King of Pentacles share with my clients?

THE PAGE OF WANDS—GIFT—CREATIVITY

Elemental Associations

Page—Earth

Wands—Fire

The Page of Wands is creativity personified. He sees creative opportunities everywhere and is the first to offer solutions and inventions that no one else has considered before. He is able to bring things forward from inspiration to form. The Page of Wands is utterly uninterested in passionless people, projects, relationships, and spiritual paths. He knows that passion is a driving force for change and creation. That is not to say that the Page of Wands hasn't been burnt by his experiences. He plays with fire of course, but he knows that everything that he touches has the power to transform. This is the gift of creativity.

Take some time to connect with the creator within you. Do you consider yourself a creative person? Why or why not? When was the last time you created something? Do you fear judgement of your creativity? Has that stopped you from fully embracing your creative side?

EXERCISE

Place the cards as follows:

1. The Page of Wands—the significator card

2. How can I ignite my creativity?

3. What is potentially blocking my creativity?

4. What is being transformed inside me?

5. What does the Page of Wands have to teach me about being a creator?

6. How can I connect to the Page of Wands better as a tarot card?

7. What lesson can the Page of Wands share with my clients?

THE KNIGHT OF WANDS—GIFT—ADVENTURE

Elemental Associations

Knight—Fire

Wands—Fire

The Knight of Wands is always on an adventure of some sort. He inspires us and enthralls crowds of people with his tales of far-off places and wild exploration. He also seems to have friends everywhere. He is an ever expanding being. The Knight of Wands can show us what a beautiful gift being open to the world, people, and experiences can be. He sees challenges and obstacles in life as just another adventure waiting to happen. He is the desire to dare within all of us and calls us to join him into the wilds to ultimately find ourselves.

Take some time to connect with your inner explorer. Do you crave adventure or the couch? (Either is cool, no judgement.) What is adventurous to you? When was the last time you explored something you were passionate about? How do you handle new experiences, people, and places?

EXERCISE

Place the cards as follows:

1. The Knight of Wands—the significator card

2. What is to be discovered for me right now?

3. What is holding me back?

4. How can I be more open to challenging the norm?

5. What does the Knight of Wands have to teach me about adventure?

6. How can I connect to the Knight of Wands better as a tarot card?

7. What lesson can the Knight of Wands share with my clients?

THE QUEEN OF WANDS–GIFT–CONFIDENCE

Elemental Associations

Queen—Water

Wands—Fire

The Queen of Wands exudes confidence and class and she demands it quietly. When the Queen of Wands walks into a room, all eyes follow her. She doesn't shy away from the limelight and enjoys being in her personal power. Even if you are not one to seek attention, the Queen of Wands holds the gift of personal inner confidence—that inner flame that doesn't ever go out and doesn't need outside sources to fuel it. It is from there that we are able to move through the world confidently. It impacts every area of our lives, from ensuring that we have healthy boundaries to standing up for ourselves and what we believe in and having self-sustaining energy and drive.

Take some time to connect with your inner flame. How brightly is it shining? How does it make you feel when you have attention on you? Do you view yourself as a confident person? How does it feel when you are in a space of confidence?

Place the cards as follows:

1. The Queen of Wands—the significator card

2. How can I bring more confidence into my life?

3. What fears do I have around being my authentic self?

4. What can I release that is no longer serving my confidence levels?

5. What guidance does the Queen of Wands have for me?

6. How can I connect to the Queen of Wands better as a tarot card?

7. What lesson can the Queen of Wands share with my clients?

THE KING OF WANDS–GIFT–LEADERSHIP

Elemental Associations

King—Air

Wands—Fire

The King of Wands is a natural-born leader. He inspires loyalty and action in people as easily as it is for the rest of us to breathe. He knows that to rally people to his cause and vision, he needs to lead through action and passion. Leadership can be quiet or full of force, but it is always inclusive. To be a real leader, you are required to take full responsibility for your life so that you can inspire those around you to work with you in realising your dreams. Leaders do not see themselves as better than anyone else, but as an essential part of a team. The King of Wands can teach us a lot about embracing our inner leader.

Take some time to connect with the leader within you. What kind of leaders inspire you? Who has been your favourite leader in your life? What kind of leader would you like to be?

EXERCISE

Place the cards as follows:

1. The King of Wands—the significator card

2. What is my style of leadership?

3. How can I inspire loyalty in others?

4. How can I manifest my vision in life?

5. What does the King of Wands have to teach me about leadership?

6. How can I connect to the King of Wands better as a tarot card?

7. What lesson can the King of Wands share with my clients?

THE PAGE OF SWORDS—GIFT—INSPIRATION

Elemental Associations

Page—Earth

Swords—Air

The Page of Swords calls down the lofty ideas and inspiration from the mind and brings them to earth. The Page of Swords is always discovering new things and new ways of looking at situations or people. He is always in a sense of awe of the magic that is all around us. When we are inspired in life, we are not only in a place of generation, but we also inspire those around us. The Page of Swords can be our muse if we let this energy into our space and listen to the music they play.

Take some time to connect with your inner muse. What inspires you? Who inspires you? What doesn't inspire you? Do you have a guide or muse that you connect and communicate with in life? How does your spiritual path inspire you?

EXERCISE

Place the cards as follows:

1. The Page of Swords—the significator card

2. What can I do to be more inspired?

3. What blocks (if any) do I have when trying to tap into my inspiration?

4. How can I be more inspiring to others?

5. What does the Page of Swords have to teach me about inspiration?

6. How can I connect to the Page of Swords better as a tarot card?

7. What lesson can the Page of Swords share with my clients?

THE KNIGHT OF SWORDS–GIFT–ACTION

Elemental Associations

Knight—Fire

Swords—Air

The Knight of Swords does not care for excuses or reasons for not moving forward. They are already doing what most people are just considering or are too busy for. The Knight of Swords is always moving and it is this energy that can help us get unstuck and move towards the place that we really want to be. While movement for movement's sake can be a type of avoidance, this knight knows the quest that he is on is one of great importance. It is the gift of acting on our passions that this card can bring to our lives.

Take some time to connect with your inner warrior. What causes are important to you? When was the last time you exercised? Do you seek outside guidance every time before you act? When was the last time you actively worked on your passion projects?

EXERCISE

Place the cards as follows:

1. The Knight of Swords—the significator card

2. What do I need to do right now in order to move forward?

3. What do I need to stop overthinking about?

4. How can I be more of a warrior in my life?

5. What does the Knight of Swords have to teach me about taking action?

6. How can I connect to the Knight of Swords better as a tarot card?

7. What lesson can the Knight of Swords share with my clients?

THE QUEEN OF SWORDS–GIFT–TRUTH

Elemental Associations

Queen—Water

Swords—Air

The Queen of Swords knows herself deeply, which makes her a formidable person indeed. Not much shakes her or can sway her when her mind is made up. The Queen of Swords can see into the truth of any matter and can be a brilliant ally in planning and self-discovery. The truth is not always easy to hear, which can earn this card quite the reputation, but the Queen of Swords knows that it is only when we come to the truth that real change can begin.

Take some time to connect with your inner truth. What do you know to be true about yourself? What has lead you to your inner truth in life? Do you fear telling or sharing the truth to those you know? Do you stand by your convictions and beside your choices when you have made them?

EXERCISE

Place the cards as follows:

1. The Queen of Swords—the significator card

2. How can I be more assertive with my inner truth?

3. What truths am I afraid of?

4. How can I let them go with love and understanding?

5. What does the Queen of Swords have to teach me about emotional intelligence?

6. How can I connect to the Queen of Swords better as a tarot card?

7. What lesson can the Queen of Swords share with my clients?

THE KING OF SWORDS—GIFT—CLARITY

Elemental Associations

King—Air

Swords—Air

The King of Swords is the expert in his given field and has been elevated to that place through crystal clarity. He does not waste time or energy on anything that would complicate matters, and he can see the world through a very defined lens. The King of Swords is known to see a situation as either black or white, and shades of grey do not interest him. While this is extreme, he can aid us in seeing straight and getting through times of confusion and drama.

Take some time to connect with your vision. What do you do when something or someone confuses you? How does it feel when you gain clarity on something? Do you speak your needs clearly to others? Do you believe in extremes when it comes to people or situations without looking at all sides of the matter?

EXERCISE

Place the cards as follows:

1. The King of Swords—the significator card

2. How can I find more clarity?

3. What is blocking my view?

4. What do I need to focus on?

5. What does the King of Swords have to teach me about decisiveness?

6. How can I connect to the King of Swords better as a tarot card?

7. What lesson can the King of Swords share with my clients?

⌣ Appendix I ⌣
TAROT COURT CARD CHEAT SHEETS

Who doesn't love a good cheat sheet? I know I do. These cheat sheets are meant to be used as a one-stop reference page for each of the court cards. Information is taken from each chapter of the book. So if you have not read the book in its entirety and something here is confusing, you may want to read that section to get up to speed. Don't worry, I won't tell on you for not reading the book from start to finish.

THE PAGE OF PENTACLES

Element: Earth

Zodiac: Any of the three earth signs—Virgo, Taurus, Capricorn

Age: Infant—11 years of age (inclusive)

Timing: Days

Season: Winter

Mantra: I do

Keywords

- Messages of the material kind (notification of a raise at work, for example)
- Earthy
- Active
- Energetic
- Kinaesthetic
- Practical
- Thrifty
- Animal Lover
- Tactile

Archetype: The Naturalist

This being feels like they are at home, surrounded by furry animals and nature. Nothing makes them happier or allows them to feel more like themselves. They want to feel the dirt in between their toes and to breathe in fresh air. Even if they are in the city, they will search for green spaces full with animals.

The Page of Pentacles is the kind of person who does well in a relationship where they are not required to make big life changing decisions and can follow the lead of someone else, for the most part. They do well in relationships and prefer them over being single, but they are also more prone to end up being a stereotypical crazy cat lady than any other tarot archetype.

While the Naturalist has all of the patience in the world, they will test everyone around them with the limit of theirs. While everyone else is running around in a panic, this tarot archetype will simply and quietly do what needs to be done in their own time. These people are often a good reminder to others that we need to slow down and connect to our bodies and the rhythms of nature more often than we probably are.

Ideal jobs for the Page of Pentacles are veterinarians or animal rescue and rehabilitation workers, animal trainers, zoologists, gardeners, landscapers, horticulturists, greenhouse specialists, and herbalists.

THE KNIGHT OF PENTACLES

Element: Earth

Zodiac: Virgo

Age: 12–21 Years (inclusive)

Timing: Weeks

Season: Winter

Mantra: I endure all in service

Keywords

- Acting through the material (building, etc.)
- Self-discovery through material things
- Practical action
- Getting a new job
- City planner
- Leaving home and town
- Endurance
- Loyalty

Archetype: The Soldier

Slightly rigid but strong as an ox, reliable as the sun rise and steady as a mountain, the Soldier is the kind of person that you want to face the zombie apocalypse with. This person has almost superhuman reserves of energy when it comes to doing things for other people, and they live to serve.

When in a relationship, the Soldier is going to give everything they have to their other half, but know that their duty to the greater good trumps even the best sex they have ever had and the family they have to leave behind while they are off saving the world.

A hard working team member for sure, this archetype may not set the business world on fire with groundbreaking new technologies or ideas but they are going to be the ones who makes sure the work gets done well. They make sure projects are delivered and that people are safe and sound.

Ideal jobs for the Knight of Pentacles, outside being an actual soldier, are any positions in the financial industry where there is detail and consistency and where they do work that a lot of people find boring. Accounting, financial planning, stockbrokering, or professional gambling (which gives them that knight-like thrill). Work with the body is also well matched for the Soldier jobs, such as being a personal trainer or nutritionist.

THE QUEEN OF PENTACLES

Element: Earth

Zodiac: Capricorn

Age: 22 Years +

Timing: Months

Season: Winter

Mantra: I nurture through the body

Keywords

- Emotionally grounded
- Lady of luxury
- Identity through belongings
- Generosity
- House proud
- Nurturing through food, cooking, and the body

- High society
- High maintenance
- Elegance

Archetype: The Healer

The Healer as a person is literally like a walking hug. You just want to be around them because they make you feel better on every level. Comfort, well-being, and safety are at the top of the Healer's list of importance. They want to make sure that the people they are around are well-fed, have a good solid roof over their heads, and are happy.

The Healer in their shadow side can be rather in denial about needing a healer themselves. This is most often the case not because they believe themselves to be infallible, but because they just spend all of their time taking care of everyone else that their needs do not come into play. When these people burn out, they usually do in a spectacular fashion and need a lot of time to build their energy reserves back up.

When in a relationship, the Healer is going to be the one who wants to fix everything for their other half. They need to be with someone who is going to give them the support and energy right back or else they are going to end up feeling used and discarded when they realise what is happening. This is an archetype who does love being in a relationship and loves children and family life.

Ideal careers for the Queen of Pentacles is anything in a profession of healing and bodywork such as doctors, nurses, midwives, massage therapists, and herbalists. The Queen of Pentacles may also find themselves gravitating towards a nurturing role such as a chef, cook, gardener, landscaper, or florist, working with the human body or the earth.

THE KING OF PENTACLES

Element: Earth

Zodiac: Taurus

Age: 22 Years +

Timing: Years

Season: Winter

Mantra: I lead with my wallet

Keywords

- Material maturity
- Money manager
- Business owner
- Stable leader
- Dominant at home
- CEO, CFO, COO
- Greed
- Stubbornness

Archetype: The Manager

There is no other tarot archetype that you would trust more with making you filthy rich than the Manager. They are dependable to the point of boredom and have an uncanny way of working with numbers, money, and large, complex systems in order to make everything work. Whether this is managing large hedge funds or running a military base or even a well-oiled home, this is the person for the job when things need structure, routine, and growth.

Everyone and everything is competition to this archetype if they are not feeling secure within their role in life. They will view everything as a threat to their success and keep everyone at arm's length or just simply take them down a peg or two.

The Manager will want a steady home and love life. They feel as though their time is better spent working than dealing with personal drama. They will provide for everyone under their roof without a second thought but may not be the most romantic of the tarot archetypes.

Ideal careers for the King of Pentacles will be anything where there is a lot of money to be gained. High-powered positions in property investment, construction, investment banking, and multibillion-dollar businesses are very alluring to this king. Other King of Pentacles positions include working as an exploration geologist or army commander.

THE PAGE OF SWORDS

Element: Air

Zodiac: Any of the three air signs—Gemini, Libra, Aquarius

Age: Infant—11 years of age (inclusive)

Timing: Days

Season: Autumn

Mantra: I ask

Keywords

- Inquisitive
- Messages of the intellectual kind
- Inspiration
- Simple solutions
- The question: why?
- Understanding
- Contemplation
- Discovery

Archetype: The Detective

Life is something to be solved to the Detective. They love to know what makes people tick, what made something happen, and how they can put the puzzle together to make sense. If they are unable to figure someone or something it out, it is going to drive them to distraction.

If the Detective does not do any personal or developmental work for themselves they will likely push everyone away from them, deeming interpersonal relationships a distraction from their real work. They do not like to know or be told what their weaknesses are as they can believe they are infallible.

Good luck trying to surprise this tarot archetype. They know all of the hidden places in their living space (and yours if they have been around you long enough) and will pick up on what you are trying to plan for them. While this may kill the romantic buzz, they will be excellent at surprising you.

"Boring" and this person do not go hand-in-hand. They will just get destructive and cause a world of problems for everyone else they work with. The Detective, if they aren't working in that field or something similar, wants a lot on their to-do list and a lot of projects on the go. The busier the better as far as they are concerned.

Ideal careers for the Page of Swords include: police force, detectives, private investigators, statisticians, spy, code crackers, language specialists, librarians, the professional student, philosopher, research aid, laboratory technician, copywriter, or editor.

THE KNIGHT OF SWORDS

Element: Air

Zodiac: Gemini

Age: 12–21 Years (inclusive)

Timing: Weeks

Season: Autumn

Mantra: I know what I do

Keywords

- Self-discovery through the intellect
- Acting on impulse
- All bark no bite
- Talking first then thinking later
- Innovation
- Cutting or hurtful words
- Charging ahead

- Rash decisions
- Immaturity

Archetype: The Warrior

The Warrior is a finely tuned machine—not only physically but mentally as well. They know that it is only half of the battle to have a body that is ready for anything; the mind has to be just as well trained.

Warriors like strong partners, but they will also likely want to be the more dominant person in their relationship. It can be because their work schedule is so demanding and they are required to move around a lot or because they just like being the one who is calling the shots. The Warrior will seek out someone who can go toe-to-toe with them on all levels.

If there are issues in a workplace that require someone to go in, change everything, mix things up, or clean up a massive mess, this is the right person for the job. Most Warriors will naturally find a line of work where they embody their archetype every day, where they are on the field—whether that is a sports field or in the field of battle. All of the roles they will want to work in require lots of movement and action.

Ideal careers for the Knight of Swords are: private investigator, stunt person, martial arts expert, law enforcement, air force, professional sports of any kind, freedom fighter, and activist.

THE QUEEN OF SWORDS

Element: Air

Zodiac: Libra

Age: 22 Years +

Timing: Months

Season: Autumn

Mantra: I nurture through the mind

Keywords

- Emotional intelligence
- Problem-solver
- Fair
- Soothing words
- Nurturing through kind words
- Always knows what to say
- Icy words
- Shock
- Manipulating words

Archetype: The Judge

You can tell this tarot archetype just about anything and they will be there to support and aid you if possible. If there is a solution, they will help you find it. Conversely, this is not a person you want to try to con. They are not about to be sweet-talked into anything and will call you out if you are acting like a clown. The Judge is a no-nonsense kind of person when it comes to the truth but that does not mean that they are uncaring.

The Judge can be harsh and cruel if they have found their heart to be hardened or are disconnected from themselves. They know exactly what buttons to push with people and will remember everything someone ever said to them, filing it away for the right time to use it to their advantage.

While it can be said that communication is key in any relationship, the Judge knows that this is what is going to make or break any pairing. They want to be with someone who is open and that they can talk to about anything. They are loyal, friendly, and fun and love to be in love.

Ideal careers for the Queen of Swords include: teacher, lecturer, ambassador, mentor, linguistic specialist, mediator, negotiator, talk show host, actress or actor, psychologist, psychiatrist, marriage counsellor, sex therapist, judge, and lawyer.

THE KING OF SWORDS

Element: Air

Zodiac: Aquarius

Age: 22 Years +

Timing: Years

Season: Autumn

Mantra: I lead with logic

Keywords

- Intellectual maturity
- Brilliant mind
- Highly educated
- Keen minded
- Tunnel vision
- Massive amounts of influence
- Logical ruler
- All in the mind

Archetype: The Scientist

The Scientist is a person on a mission. They feel it in their bones that they can change the world for the better if only they are given the chance. They are naturally drawn to books, reading, education, and learning as much as they possibly can from an early age. The Scientist can be an intimidating person but they rarely lord their accomplishments over other people or want to make others feel insignificant.

This tarot archetype is going to excel at anything they put their mind to. Anything. If they want to write a doctorate and get their PhD, they will. If they want to work on curing a disease, they will. If they want to make radical social change, they will. This is where this archetype shines, when they are doing their work in the world.

The Scientist would love nothing more than to find someone who can talk the language of their chosen field. Debating theories and working out problems is pretty much foreplay. The more they can make them think, the sexier it is for them. Their other half will not always feel as though they come first, because in reality they don't. The work does, but they do love strongly.

Ideal jobs for the King of Swords include scientists in all fields, mathematicians, lawmakers, legislators, lawyers, attorneys general, IT professionals, politicians, inventor, professors, surgeons, or doctors.

THE PAGE OF WANDS

Element: Fire

Zodiac: Any of the three fire signs—Aries, Leo, Sagittarius

Age: Infant—11 years of age (inclusive)

Timing: Days

Season: Summer

Mantra: I create

Keywords

- Messages of the spiritual or creative kind
- Synchronicity
- Creative solutions
- Creative people
- Messy people
- Impish
- Cheeky
- Mischievous
- Imaginative

Archetype: Peter Pan

This charming tarot archetype is sweet as pie as long as they are getting their own way and can live a carefree life. They live to be at ease and to enjoy as much of life as possible. Pleasure is their middle name.

As soon as things get too real or they are being asked to be held accountable for something in their lives, they are likely to throw down a smoke bomb and disappear magician-style rather than face the music.

If Peter Pan has done no personal development work, they are in for a life of frustrated family members, lovers, and co-workers. Any time something goes wrong, they think it is never their fault, and that is going to grow old for everyone else around them.

Peter Pan will love to explore lots of different careers and hobbies and will put all of their energy into their current flavour of the month. When it gets too hard, they simply jump to the next thing. This does mean that they are versatile and full of information that would make them an asset at any quiz night.

Ideal careers for the Page of Wands are any career that is aligned with the suit of the wands. This archetype is more likely to jump from career to career than any other. They have a real "screw the man" mentality about work and money and may struggle with long-term responsibilities of any kind.

The Knight of Wands

Element: Fire

Zodiac: Sagittarius

Age: 12–21 Years (inclusive)

Timing: Weeks

Season: Summer

Mantra: I will clear the path

Keywords
- Creative action
- Spiritual seeker
- Going on an adventure

- Saying yes
- Self-discovery
- Travel
- Doing things on impulse
- Exploration

Archetype: The Adventurer

Oh the places that this person is going to go… This is a truly independent being who is happy as long as they are able to say they are learning or doing something new today and tomorrow. The Adventurer wants to push their own boundaries when it comes to trying new foods, learning a new language, getting that promotion, and experiencing new lovers.

If the Adventurer has not done any self-development work, they are likely to be selfish and egotistical, looking down at people who prefer a life with routine and stability. They run away from problems and do not like the idea of their pasts catching up with them, because that would be messy.

They are excellent when it comes to thinking outside the box or when you need someone to solve a problem that seems impossible. They will push those around them outside of their comfort zones and inspire others to blaze their own trails.

Ideal careers for the Knight of Wands include those of backpackers, extreme sports persons, firefighters, stunt people, tour guides, hospitality personnel, travel guides, travel writers or bloggers, couch surfer, party planners, wedding planners, pilots, and yogis.

THE QUEEN OF WANDS

Element: Fire

Zodiac: Aries

Age: 22 Years +

Timing: Months

Season: Summer

Mantra: I nurture through the soul

Keywords

- Spiritual and soulful person
- Communicating through spirit
- Temper
- Spiritual mentor
- Warm person
- Spiritual nurturing
- Flamboyant
- Aggressive

Archetype: The Performer

Spotlight, please. Actually, this person is a living, breathing spotlight, so they rarely need extra lighting but they won't say no to the extra attention. There is always an opportunity for the Performer to share their talents with the world. They live to surprise and delight everyone around them and they truly light up any room when they are given the opportunity to express themselves.

A performer in their shadow side is going to be impossible to get to know as they move from one personality and performance to another. They tell different people different stories about their lives and they do not like people really knowing who they are.

The Performer needs to be the star of the show in a relationship. They want to know that they are the number one priority. It can be a struggle for their significant others. They will want someone who can go to every gallery opening and award night and be happy to allow them to shine. They want someone who is proud to be with them.

Ideal careers for the Queen of Wands include the actress and actor that their archetype is named after. They are also suited to PR work, HR work, being a professional socialite, campaign manager, fashion designer, or pop star.

THE KING OF WANDS

Element: Fire

Zodiac: Aries

Age: 22 Years +

Timing: Years

Season: Summer

Mantra: I lead with passion

Keywords

- Spiritual maturity
- Leading through creativity
- Leading through spirituality
- Church/religious leaders
- Fanatic
- Cult leader
- Charismatic
- Politician
- Passionate leader

Archetype: The Entrepreneur

This is the kind of person who is going to have their photo on the cover of *Time* magazine, have movies made about their life story, and not even know what the word "no" means when it comes to their life goals. This person will take risks and make gambles that would make most people incredibly uncomfortable, but more often than not, they pay off big time.

The Entrepreneur in the shadow side will crush anyone they need to in order to get ahead in life. They don't see people, they just see resources and will without question take what they want to get them to the next level in their life and business.

This archetype needs a life and business partner, not just a romantic one. They will be in control of the relationship and major decisions so they require an element of compliance from their other half. They also want that person to believe in what they are doing as this is a deal breaker for them.

Ideal careers for the King of Wands include titles like CEO, business owner, director, chairman, entrepreneur, manager, and president. People who work in consulting or have start-ups are often aligned with this archetype. Self-employed people of all kinds are this archetype as well.

THE PAGE OF CUPS

Element: Water

Zodiac: Any of the three water signs—Cancer, Pisces, Scorpio

Age: Infant—11 years of age (inclusive)

Timing: Days

Season: Spring

Mantra: I feel

Keywords

- Messages of the emotional kind
- Naivety
- Unconditional love
- Simple emotion
- Daydreamer
- Sensitive
- New babies or pregnancy

Archetype: The Empath

The Empath is the emotional and energetic gauge for the environment they are in. They will be able to sense what is going on in an instant and they are VERY hard to mislead as they know what is really going on. While they are extremely sensitive, this is not something that is a weakness; it is a true gift—especially when it is honed into something that works in their favour.

This archetype can often find it hard to speak up at work or in a relationship because they have a lot of conflicting feelings (not all of them theirs either) going on within them and around them. They love being with other people, especially those few who truly understand them and allow them to be themselves.

Small businesses that allow this archetype to set their own schedules are perfect for this archetype because they can manage their energy better. This is not to say that Empaths are unable to work in larger businesses or conventional office spaces, but they tend to thrive more when they are allowed to control who they invite into their energetic space and for how long.

Ideal careers for the Page of Cups is any career that is aligned with working with creative energy and art: painter, poet, writer, actor, sculptor, dancer, visual artist.

THE KNIGHT OF CUPS

Element: Water

Zodiac: Pisces

Age: 12–21 Years (inclusive)

Timing: Weeks

Season: Spring

Mantra: Love is the highest power

Keywords

- Acts on emotions
- Self-discovery through love
- Self-discovery through emotions
- Poet
- Casanova

- Infatuation
- Service to love

Archetype: The Romantic

Hold on to your headboard, you are in for one wild ride when it comes to this archetype. If you are looking for someone to wrap you up in their world and make you feel special then look no further than the Romantic. They will wine and dine you like nobody else can. Just don't expect them to give you a copy of their apartment key.

If the Romantic is not self-aware, they will leave a string of broken hearts and pissed off exs and friends behind them. Emotional collateral is high with these shadow Romantics. They simply take what they want and leave.

This is a truly expressive and creative soul who is usually into many art forms. They love to work with mediums of all kinds and will surround themselves with beautiful things. They care about the social and personal image and feel as though they have a role to uphold—one they cherish.

Ideal careers for the Knight of Cups/Romantic include artistic endeavours of all kinds: graphic design, visual design, photographers, poets, actors, singers, tattoo artists, writer, dancers.

THE QUEEN OF CUPS

Element: Water

Zodiac: Cancer

Age: 22 Years +

Timing: Months

Season: Spring

Mantra: I nurture through love and emotions

Keywords

- Emotional person
- Emotional poise

- Caregiver

- Nurturing

- Passive power

- Emotionally manipulative

- Drama queen

- Self-sacrificing

Archetype: The Mystic

There are two words you can use to sum up this archetype: mysterious and magical. There is something that you just can't put your finger on with this person, and they like it that way. They are a walking spiritual ham radio.

If they are struggling with their own shadow side, they will turn on the water works to get their way and go from emotionally boiling to arctic freeze in seconds.

They crave true acceptance more than anything from their significant other and will likely hide their intuitive talents until they feel safe to share that most intimate part of themselves with their lovers and even family.

Ideal careers for the Queen of Cups include therapist, counsellor, midwife, doula, doctor, nurse, naturopath, herbalist, osteopath, shaman, witch, tarot reader, social worker, and medium.

THE KING OF CUPS

Element: Water

Zodiac: Scorpio

Age: 22 Years +

Timing: Years

Season: Spring

Mantra: I lead with my heart

Keywords

- Maturity

- Emotionally strong

- Emotional ruler

- Head of the family

- Sensitive New Age Person

- Lack of Sympathy

- Cut off from emotions

Archetype: Hades

Deep and considerate. This archetype can look into the depths of your soul with one glance. They want to explore all aspects of life and are not afraid to tackle often taboo subjects or areas of work.

If they have not done any of their own personal work or shadow work, they are likely to be someone who deflects and manipulates. They can even just be flat out cruel.

They love intensely and completely and will do just about anything for the people they adore. Their family is the most important thing to them. Once crossed or betrayed, they are very hard to get forgiveness from.

Ideal/possible careers for the King of Cups include doctor, humanitarian, therapist, psychologist, philosopher, artist, spiritual leader, mortician, or palliative care worker.

BIBLIOGRAPHY

Banzhaf, Hanjo. *Tarot and the Journey of the Hero*. York Beach: Weiser, 2000.

Browning, Frank. *The Fate of Gender, Nature, Nurture, and the Human Future*. New York: Bloomsbury, 2016.

Butler, Bill. *The Definitive Tarot*. London: Rider and Company, 1975.

Cabot, Laurie & Cowan, Tom. *Love Magic*. London: Pan Books, 1992.

Callahan, Gerald N. *Between XX and XY Intersexuality and the Myth of Two Sexes*. Chicago: Chicago Review Press, 2009.

Campbell, Joseph. *The Hero with a Thousand Faces*. Novato, CA: New World Library, 2008.

Case, Paul Foster. *The Tarot: A Key to the Wisdom of the Ages*. New York: Penguin, 2006.

Crowley, Aleister. *Thoth Tarot Deck*. Stamford, CT: U.S. Games Systems Inc., 2005.

Daniels, Kooch N. & Daniels, Victor. *Tarot D'Amour*. York Beach, ME: Weiser, 2003.

Douglas, Alfred. *The Tarot*. New York: Penguin, 1972.

Echols, Signe E. MS., Mueller, Robert, Ph.D. and Thomson, Sandra A. *Spiritual Tarot*. New York: William Morrow Paperbacks, 1996.

Fenton-Smith, Paul. *The Tarot Revealed*. Crows Nest, N.S.W.: Allen & Unwin, 2008.

Fenton-Smith, Paul. *Tarot Masterclass*. Crows Nest, N.S.W.: Allen & Unwin, 2007.

Goodman, Linda. *Linda Goodman's Love Signs*. New York: Ballantine Books, 1978.

Grimal, Pierre. *The Penguin Dictionary of Classical Mythology*. London: Penguin, 1991.

Hasbrouch, Muriel Bruce. *Tarot and Astrology*. Rochester, VT: Destiny Books, 1996.

Jung, C.G. *The Archetypes and The Collective Unconscious*. New York: Princeton University Press, 1981.

———*Psychology of the Unconscious: A Study of the Transformations and Symbolisms of the Libido: A Contribution to the History of the Evolution of Thought*. New York: Princeton Univ. Pr., 1991.

Krans, Kim. *The Wild Unknown Tarot*. San Francisco: HarperOne, 2016.

Laurence, Theodor. *The Sexual Key to the Tarot*. Charleston, SC: CreateSpace Independent Publishing Platform, 2017.

Lindsey, Linda L. *Gender Roles: A Sociological Perspective*. New York: Routledge, 2016.

Louis, Anthony. *Tarot Plain and Simple*. St. Paul, MN: Llewellyn Worldwide, 1996.

Morgan, Ffiona. *Daughters of the Moon Tarot*. Willits, CA: Daughters of the Moon, 1986.

Nichols, Sallie. *Jung and Tarot: An Archetypal Journey*. San Francisco: Weiser, 1980.

Nicolson, Harold George. *Kings, Courts and Monarchy*. New York: Simon and Schuster. 1962.

O'Neill, Robert V. *Tarot Symbolism*. Lima, OH: Fairway Press, 2004.

Ozaniec, Naomi. *The Watkins Tarot Handbook*. London: Watkins Publishing, 2005.

Place, Robert M. *The Tarot; History, Symbolism and Divination*. London: Penguin, 2005.

Pollack, Rachel. *Seventy-Eight Degrees of Wisdom*. London: Weiser, 2009.

Pollack, Rachel. *The New Tarot Handbook*. Woodbury, MN: Llewellyn Worldwide, 2012.

Prosapio, Richard. *Intuitive Tarot*. Stamford, CT: U.S. Games Systems, 2003.

Rosengarten, Arthur, Ph.D. *Tarot and Psychology*. St. Paul: Paragon House, 2000.

Telesco, Patricia. *Mirror, Mirror: Reflections of the Sacred Self*. Sun Lakes, AZ: Blue Star Productions, 1999.

Urnash, Egypt. *Tarot of the Silicon Dawn*. Woodbury, MN: Lo Scarabeo, 2011.

Vega, Phyllis. *Romancing the Tarot*. New York: Fireside, 2001.

Waite, Arthur E. *The Pictorial Key to the Tarot*. Stamford, CT: U.S. Games Systems Inc., 1989.

Woolfolk, Joanna Martine. *The Only Astrology Book You'll Ever Need*. Plymouth, UK: Taylor Trade Publishing, 2012.

An all-new approach!

Tarot

For Beginners

A Practical Guide to Reading the Cards

THE HIGH PRIESTESS

BARBARA MOORE

Tarot for Beginners
A Practical Guide to Reading the Cards
Barbara Moore

Tarot for Beginners makes it easier than ever to learn all you need to know about reading the cards. Award-winning tarot expert Barbara Moore provides a complete foundation in tarot, clearly explaining each aspect while encouraging you to develop your own unique reading style.

Begin with the history and myths behind tarot and discover the meanings of all seventy-eight cards—broken down into suit, number, and major and minor arcana for simpler learning. You'll also explore symbols, reversals, spreads, interpretation techniques, tarot journaling, and more.

Sample readings of predictive, prescriptive, interactive, and intuitive styles will also help you give insightful and fulfilling readings for yourself and others.

978-0-7387-1955-9, 360 pp., 5³⁄₁₆ x 8 $15.95

To order, call 1-877-NEW-WRLD or visit llewellyn.com
Prices subject to change without notice

Tarot Reversals for Beginners
Five Approaches to Reading Upside-Down Cards
Leeza Robertson

Many people don't know what to do when a card appears upside down in a tarot spread. This book helps you become more comfortable and confident when these topsy-turvy cards dance into your readings. Join author Leeza Robertson as she explores five distinct areas of energy related to reversals: blocks, protection, mirror, shadow, and retrograde. This system of reading reversals is a simple way to deepen your connection to the cards and receive the guidance they have to offer.

978-0-7387-5271-6, 360 pp., 5¼ x 8   **$16.99**

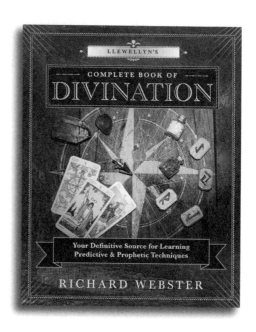

Llewellyn's Complete Book of Divination
Your Definitive Source for Learning Predictive & Prophetic Techniques
RICHARD WEBSTER

Richard Webster, one of the world's bestselling new age authors, explores the incredibly wide variety of divination systems from around the world. Discover in-depth information and how-to instruction for more than thirty divination practices, including:

Tarot • Astrology • Palmistry • Numerology • Pendulums • I Ching • Automatic Writing • Candle Reading • Coin Divination • Flower Reading • Dowsing • Runes • Scrying • Geomancy • Bibliomancy • And Much More

Llewellyn's Complete Book of Divination also features helpful tips for choosing the best form of divination for your specific needs and preparation methods to practice before a divination session. Learn about the history of divination and the historical figures who could see the future. Find out how raising your intuitive skills can improve nearly every aspect of your life, from relationships and health to money and career. Whether you're just getting started or are a seasoned expert, this thorough guide holds sacred wisdom and wonderful surprises for you.

978-0-7387-5175-7, 360 pp., 8 x 10 $29.99

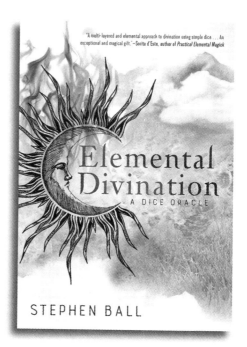

"A multi-layered and elemental approach to divination using simple dice . . . An exceptional and magical gift."—Sorita d'Este, author of *Practical Elemental Magick*

Elemental Divination

A DICE ORACLE

STEPHEN BALL

Elemental Divination
A Dice Oracle
STEPHEN BALL

Discover a simple practice that yields life-changing results. With just three dice, you can receive answers to basic questions or initiate a deeper interpretive journey. Based on elemental forces that have been consulted by healers and sages for thousands of years, this dice oracle will inspire you to see yourself and the world with a whole new perspective.

This book shares instructions and rituals for using the oracle with dice or other divinatory tools. You will also find a list of meanings for every possible elemental combination and explanations of how Earth, Air, Fire, Water, Sun, and Moon manifest in this divination system. When you explore the oracle's patterns and correspondences, you gain insight into the challenges and concerns that we all face. Integrate the power of the elements as you make your way through the magic and mystery of life with *Elemental Divination* as your guide.

978-0-7387-5447-5, 240 pp., 5 x7   **$15.99**